Minnesota Memories

by Joan Claire Graham and Kathy A.Megyeri

Introduction

The stories in this collection are about real, not fictional people, places and events. If you are from Minnesota, you will recognize kindred spirits and familiar settings. Whether you grew up in Cloquet or Kiester, St. Cloud, Lake City or Pipestone, these *Minnesota Memories* will trigger your recollection of similar memories.

Family jealousy and secrets, eccentric relatives, cherished memorabilia, neighborhood kids and pets, school days, church events, hospitality, town celebrations, dreams gone awry, social expectations and taboos, hero worship, and pragmatic pronounce-ments from mothers who categorized material possessions as "ev-ery day" or "good," --all are part of our collective memory of life in the North Star State.

This volume of *Minnesota Memories* consists of two parts. Part I contains reflections of a single author from Albert Lea, and Part II contains a collection of memories by seven writers from various parts of the state. Told with humor and pathos, these stories not only ring true, but they capture the essence of a place held dear by the tellers. If you've never lived in Minnesota, don't put this book down. What the heck? Even if you're from Iowa or Wisconsin, we think you'll enjoy *Minnesota Memories.*

Minnesota Memories
Table of Contents

Thanks to the following writers:

>Margaret Steele Johnson
>Jennifer Laura Paige
>Sharon McClintock Johnson
>Russell L. Christianson
>Maxine Peterson Sweatt
>Graham Frear

Thanks to the following for their help and support:

George Lanik
Stephanie Frank
Linda Evenson at the Freeborn County Historical Society
Jennifer and Phil at Signature Books
Val Farmer, "The Farmer's Forum" Fargo, ND, Column
All those Minnesotans whose stories we told

Cover photo by Aquinata " Cookie" Graham

IBSN 0-9711971-0-5

Toyota City
by Joan Claire Graham

Having lived in several parts of the country, I am always impressed by the patience and courtesy shown by my fellow Minnesotans. A situation that would evoke rude displays of impatience or sarcasm in California, New York, or the District of Columbia is most likely to be handled with down-to-earth courtesy and respect by residents of the North Star State. No situation exemplifies this theory more than what I consider one of my most embarrassing encounters with a man from a retail establishment.

As my daughter Susannah approached her second birthday in 1981, I searched for the perfect gift. She was old enough to appreciate a special surprise, but as a second child, she had already inherited her sister's toys. She didn't actually need anything new, but I'm a firm believer in making children's birthdays memorable and magical. Although our house looked like a testing ground for Toys R Us, we had never purchased a coaster wagon, so that's what I decided to buy Susannah for her second birthday.

Since it was mid-August, many stores were clearing out their wheel toys to make room for sleds and skates. Consequently, I was happy and relieved to find one remaining wagon--the kind with wooden sides--on sale at Target.

Because it was the floor model, the red and beige beauty was already assembled, which I considered a stroke of luck. As I pulled the wagon up to the cashier, however, the right rear wheel came off the axle and rolled down the aisle. Although I retrieved the wheel and tried to find the missing part, I could not find the little red cap that held the wheel on the axle.

A helpful manager told me that the part had probably been missing for quite some time. He said that Target didn't stock wagon parts, but suggested I try other stores. For some reason, I decided then and there to refer to the missing part as a hubcap.

Oh well, I thought, Susannah's only two years old. She probably won't notice it's missing, and by the time she does notice, I'll have somehow replaced the hubcap.

I brought the wagon home and loaded it with smaller gifts sent by family and friends. What a beautiful sight it was! Susannah was delighted when she came down the stairs the next morning and spent some time giving the cats rides around the house. As miraculous as it seems, the wheel stayed in place despite the missing hubcap. Of course, Susannah decided she wanted to take her new toy out for a spin, which seemed like a reasonable request for the birthday girl to make.

Susannah looked like a little princess sitting in her pretty wagon, wearing her birthday dress, holding her new stuffed dog and waving to her little friends as I pulled her along the shaded sidewalk that perfect August morning in Robbinsdale. But as we approached the sidewalk ramp to cross 38th, the rear right wheel slid off the axle and rolled down the street. I parked the wagon, shagged the wheel, and pushed it as far onto the axle as it would go. Although I walked slowly and hoped the incident would not recur, my hopes were dashed every fifty yards or so. We had to cut the birthday parade short when the wheel got loose a fifth time and was almost crushed by a car. Susannah was disappointed.

When we returned from the walk, I pointed out the missing hubcap and promised Susannah I would get a new one as soon as possible. In the meantime, we would play it safe and restrict wagon use to the play room.

In the concerned flurry of a mother on a mission to please her birthday girl, I checked the phone book. Where should I start, I wondered. Hardware stores? Toy stores? In those days, businesses were listed in the white pages along with residential numbers, and under the "T," I found what I thought would be the perfect listing--Toy City. With a name like that, I figured they must either have the part in stock or know where I could get it.

Grabbing the phone with one hand, I put my other finger under the listed phone number and dialed as quickly as possible. The problem was that in my frenzied state, my finger slipped a little, and I dialed the next number in the listing, which was Toyota City. A shot of static drowned out the voice of the person who answered the phone. I heard "Toy" and I heard "City." I had no reason to suspect I had dialed the wrong number.

"My daughter received a wagon for her birthday, and we've been having a problem with it," I began.

"I'll connect you with the service department," a friendly sounding woman said.

"Wow," I thought. "Some toy store. They have a service department. How did I get so lucky on my first try?"

"This is Al. How can I help you?" came a man's voice over the phone.

"My daughter received a wagon for her birthday, and we've been having a problem with it," I repeated.

"What seems to be the problem?" asked Al.

"Well, I replied, "One of the hubcaps is missing, and the wheel keeps falling off."

"Ma'm," Al explained patiently, "a missing hubcap does not cause the wheel to fall off."

"Sure it does," I explained. "None of the other wheels fall off. Every time the wheel falls off, I have to chase down the street to get it back, and my daughter is very disappointed."

This got Al's attention. "You've been chasing wheels down the street?" he asked.

"Yes," I said. "I have to. I know it's probably not life-threatening because when the one falls off, we still have three wheels to roll on, but it's very inconvenient to be losing that fourth wheel all the time, and it takes the joy out of the trip. "

I could tell by Al's tone of voice that he was perplexed and concerned. "What are you usually doing just before the wheel falls off?"

"Well, it almost always happens when we drive off curbs, but it has also happened on the straightaway."

"Driving off curbs?" questioned Al. "Why are you driving off curbs?"

"We have to," I explained. "It's the only way we can get where we want to go." In my mind I was wondering why Al was being so dim-witted. I can now only imagine what Al was wondering about me.

"This is very strange," he observed. The presence or absence of a hubcap has nothing to do with the stability of the wheel on the axle."

Figuring Al was hopelessly and irreversibly dense, I decided to skip ahead and ask for the wagon part I needed.

"Can you at least sell me a new hubcap or tell me where I can buy one?"

"Sure," said Al, still sounding like the perfect gentleman. "What kind of wagon is it?"

"A Radio Flyer," I answered.

After a slight pause Al replied, "We don't service those here. This is Toyota City."

I rolled my eyes back and felt the blood rush to my head as I started to physically and psychologically experience the utter embarrassment caused by the stupidity of this conversation.

"OK, thanks," I managed, as I hung up the phone and started to look for the nearest dunce cap.

Accepting my humiliation, I phoned Toy City, and got the address of the Radio Flyer company which sent the little red hubcap in a padded envelope a few days later.

I said nothing about my conversation with Al until one day when the absurdity of it came back to me in a wave that triggered non-stop laughter until my family started considering calling the men in white coats to take me away. When I was finally able to retell the tale, they shared my laughter until tears rolled down everyone's cheeks.

I can imagine that a similarly hilarious retelling had already taken place over at Al's house and at Toyota City. What made this incident such a treasured comical memory was that Al behaved like such a perfect gentleman throughout this absurd conversation. What a champ! Good comedy requires a good straight man, and Al's natural instincts framed the incident to perfection.

Al, wherever you are, I hope you did well at Toyota City, that they named you Employee of the Year, and that the guys in the service department enjoyed your retelling of your phone conversation with the crazy woman from Robbinsdale that day in 1981.

For God's Sake, Don't Tell the Klostermans
by Joan Claire Graham

The parameters of my mother's world were unbelievably narrow. She lived her last thirty some years in a Minnesota town with a population of about 14,000. She never drove a car, choosing instead to either pay fifty cents for a taxi, try to finagle a ride with a friend, or simply stay home. She seldom walked anywhere. Since she didn't drive, she didn't grocery shop. My dad picked up groceries on his way home from work, and she tolerantly made do with whatever kind of food he brought home. She didn't read very much, and aside from the "Tonight Show" and "Sing Along With Mitch," I can't think of a television program she liked to watch. She attended very few movies. In fact, there was a seven year dry spell between "The Miracle at Fatima" and "Psycho" when she didn't see any movies at all. "Psycho" was a poor comeback choice because it affected her so deeply she refused to ever take another shower.

My mother washed clothes every Monday, ironed every Tuesday, and scrubbed floors every Wednesday. She lived in fear that some remote corner of our house would be less than spotless, and an inspector from the outside would somehow come in, take notice, and make her the topic of ridicule. She and a few neighbors gathered in little picnic table klatches all summer drinking lemonade and talking about who put out a nice wash and who didn't. Those who didn't were held in contempt by the others. Those who did, put forth extraordinary effort in their dingy basement laundry rooms in order to maintain their inner circle status.

On the first Thursday of every month from September through June, Mother's bridge club got together. Ten bridge players, three of whom were named Florence, drew names to determine which month each of them would host the get-together. Somebody was usually unable to come, and on those odd occasions when all ten did show up, the extra two would rotate turns and cackle about diets or how uncomfortable their girdles were.

Refreshments, served at the end of the evening, always consisted of a five thousand calorie dessert and coffee. I always hoped to eat a piece of the rich concoction my mother inevitably made, but it never happened. A chorus of "Well I really shouldn't!" kept my hopes alive, but it was just a tease that preceded their consumption of every last crumb. Everybody clucked and cooed about how cute Mom's homemade tallies were before they took them home to show somebody. Members of the bridge club were all women my mom had met through her work in the Rosary Society, a church organization that met on Sunday nights.

Friday was clean sheet day, and we followed a system. Every sleeper was issued one clean sheet and a set of pillow cases. Before leaving for school, we would strip our beds, move the old top sheet to the bottom and wrap it around the mattress with perfect hospital corners, then put the clean sheet on the top, insert pillows into clean cases, and make the bed. Every other Friday night, we observed Catholic dietary rules with macaroni and cheese. On alternating Fridays, Mom challenged our arterial stamina with a hot dish consisting of one can of oil-packed tuna, one bag of crushed potato chips, some milk, a few token peas, and a can of cream of mushroom soup all mixed together and baked at 350 degrees for one hour.

Every Saturday, it was my responsibility to empty the kitchen silverware drawer and wash it thoroughly. I carry on this tradition today by cleaning my own silverware drawer every Saturday when there's a solar eclipse. Another Saturday activity I remember was smuggling illegal margarine from Iowa. Minnesota dairy farmers had successfully promoted a law prohibiting the sale of colored margarine, and the uncolored kind looked unappetizingly like lard. But the Iowa border was only sixteen miles from our front door, so while I scrubbed the silverware drawer, my mom or dad would enlist the interest and support of a few friends in order to justify the purchase of a case of contraband colored margarine. The conspiracy would be hatched, and within an hour, somebody would return from a short trip to Iowa with twenty-four pounds of the good stuff. This is the closest my mom came to living on the wild side.

After graduating from high school with a class of sixteen, my mother studied music and theatre at MacPhail's conservatory. For a year after graduating, she toured the East Coast directing plays, a fact documented in an old brown scrapbook filled with yellowed newsprint resplendent with glowing reviews.

But when the Great Depression started, Mother's adventures stopped. After scraping along for a few years on fifteen dollars a week directing children's plays at the library for the WPA, she married a man who worked as a government inspector in a slaughter house. Not having experienced the finer things in life, he acted as if they didn't exist, and she ran out of energy trying to convince him that they did. In time, she figured out a way to cope. She followed a regimen, and she did common tasks very well. Nobody could fault her achievements within her narrow world. She was thrifty, she kept a clean house, she sewed her own clothes and embroidered beautiful designs on dish towels, she darned socks, her children were polite, and she put out a nice wash.

On the other side of town lived her only sister, Lex Klosterman. Lex was ten years younger than my mom, and I guess you could say she was a horse of a different color.   Married to her high school sweetheart, Lex appeared to have a little pizzazz in her life. She went dancing on Saturday nights while Mom went down to the basement and worked feverishly with a brush and bleach to get the blood stains out of Dad's white slaughterhouse coveralls.

Lex's kids had all the latest toys, and Lex went to movies, bought cute clothes, lived in a new house, and took expensive vacations. Lex spent money at the beauty shop, and she and her husband traded in their old car for a new one every three years. It had nothing to do with a financial discrepancy between our two families because Lex's husband worked side by side with my dad at the slaughterhouse. Lex possessed impulsiveness in contrast to Mom's obsessively practical restraint. Lex was a doer while Mom was a dreamer.

Mom would often relate her dreams to me as we stood at the double sink after dinner. She always insisted on washing the dishes, and I dried them according to her approved method--using a beautifully embroidered white dish towel she'd made from a flour sack.

"I'd like to get new Early American furniture for the living room, but for God's sake, don't tell the Klostermans."

"Why not?"

"Because if you tell the Klostermans, then they'll run out and buy new furniture."

It was true; if Mom mentioned any idea or intention that sounded remotely interesting to the Klostermans, they would beat her to the punch. I don't suppose it occurred to them that this caused my mom so much irritation. If, in one of their daily phone conversations, my mom would mention a sale at Sears, Lex would jump into her car and go check it out. I don't think she did it for spite, but rather to satisfy her impulsive curiosity. There weren't too many entertainment options in our town, and Lex had the physical as well as the psychological mobility that Mom lacked. While Mom thought about new furniture, Lex was at the store picking out upholstery fabric.

Eventually, as the years wore on, "For God's sake, don't tell the Klostermans" replaced "Don't chew with your mouth open" as the most often repeated imperative sentence in our home--a rider tacked on to a large percentage of declarative sentences, another restriction in my already repressive existence. By stating that the shroud of secrecy was necessary "for God's sake," my mom gave daily trivia an importance it certainly didn't deserve. Compliance with this illogical conspiracy of withholding classified information from the Klostermans--for God's sake--caused me to mentally compartmentalize every topic of conversation, an exercise that put a considerable strain on the limits of my intellect and memory.

"They have canned corn-- four cans for a dollar at Piggly Wiggly, but for God's sake, don't tell the Klostermans."

"If you behave yourselves, we'll drive down to the A & W tonight for a root beer, but for God's sake, don't tell the Klostermans."

"Your dad is driving to Iowa Saturday to pick up a case of margarine, but for God's sake, don't tell the Klostermans."

I heard that phrase so often it was hard to come up with anything legal to talk about whenever we got together with the Klostermans--which was about three times a week. They were, after all, our closest relatives.

It all seems so funny in retrospect, but I suppose not telling the Klostermans was Mom's way of trying to maintain her individuality or self-esteem within those narrow parameters she had boxed herself into. Guarding her plans as if they were gold was her way of feeling there was something special or unique about her ordered existence. The Klostermans probably lived the kind of life she would have liked to have led, and their adventures and flexibility emphasized the dreariness of Mom's routine.

I did tell the Klostermans about all this many years later, and we all had a melancholy chuckle as we tried in vain to make sense of everything. Mom never changed her ways, nor did she ever schedule time for self revelation, so when she died, we were left with puzzle pieces--lots to ponder and question, but no clear explanations or answers.

School Days
by Joan Claire Graham

It was the fifties, a time of prosperity and peace following World War II and preceding Viet Nam. Many aspects of American culture were on the cusp of dramatic change, but we didn't know that. And even after television and rock and roll started to alter the way Americans spent their time, we failed to think of those changes as significant. Today I am perplexed by people who admire and glorify the fifties, for I missed most of the poodle-skirted, pony-tailed fun everybody was supposedly having. I associate living through that era with repression and austerity. You see, in addition to living in a small Minnesota town, my family was Catholic, and the only thing more oppressive than being a Catholic back then in that town was going to the Catholic school.

The public school kids told wild stories among themselves about the weird goings-on at the Catholic school (some of which were true), and they taunted us on the streets with cries of "Cat-licker, Cat-licker!" In retaliation, we would reply to those public school kids with equally shrill but angry cries of "Pup-licker, Pup-licker!" The main difference was that to them this verbal combat was fun, but to us it was a sin. Trying to figure out how to tell this in confession without invoking a lot of embarrassing questions from the priest required creativity. "I lost my temper with a Prot-estant" worked pretty well for me most of the time.

The Franciscan sisters did a pretty good job of convincing us that we were the Chosen People. They told us we had been care-fully selected by God to represent Truth in our small, predomi-nantly Scandinavian community where approximately 85% of the citizens blindly and ignorantly followed the beliefs of Martin Luther and sent their children to public schools. It appeared that the pub-lic school kids were having a lot more fun than we ever dreamed of having at St. Theodore's, but in fact those children were enjoy-ing their last few decades before spending an eternity in hell or purgatory, where they would be sent for not seeing the Truth. It was our job, as little missionaries and soldiers of Christ, to pray and work for their conversion to the One True Church.

The primary source of information about the oneness and truth of Catholicism was Father McGuire's New Baltimore Catechism, a critical part of the curriculum. Father McGuire's chapter format started with a short lesson consisting of a paragraph explaining a sacrament, church history, the nature of sin or whatever, followed by related questions with answers we had to memorize, followed by some story problems involving hypothetical situations.

In order to solve these hypothetical problems, the young Catholic had to have memorized the answers to the chapter's questions and had to apply the memorized information to the hypothetical situations. There were no shades of gray. Every problem had a right answer. Critical thinking was something that could get you tossed into purgatory, if not hell. Look where it got Martin Luther. Our job was to solve the problems, not to raise any additional questions.

The problems were like this: Mary Frances was returning from confession where she had confessed all her sins, received absolution, and performed her penance. On the way home, she passed a movie theater where posters advertised a film that had been rated "B" by the Legion of Decency. Mary Frances stopped to admire the salacious posters and was contemplating lying to her mother and attending the "B" rated film with her friends when a car hopped the curb, hit Mary Frances, and killed her. Question: Would Mary Frances' soul go straight to heaven, or would she be put into purgatory because she had been contemplating lying and attending an impure film at the time of her death?

Answer: The movie poster was a "Near Occasion of Sin." We should avoid near occasions of sin--whatever it takes. Cross the street. Look the other way. Satan (and the Lutherans) were constantly putting these roadblocks in our way to test our mettle. Since Mary Frances had not had time to reject those sinful temptations nor had she actually committed the contemplated sins, she would be able to squeak through the pearly gates. But let this be a lesson to all. It was a good thing the car didn't hop that curb five seconds later when Mary Frances had actually made up her mind to commit those two sins. Of course, if she had walked home on another street, she could have avoided those tempting movie posters AND the nasty incident with the car.

Guilt was the thing. We were always guilty. You see, we could commit a sin by thought, word or deed--by commission or omission. The only way to lead a decent life was to memorize answers, wear blinders, ask no questions and think no thoughts. And even then, you were probably guilty of something. Guilt was the most important component of education at good old St. Theodore's School.

St. Theodore's Catholic School had been built in the twenties, and I doubt that any capital improvements had ever been made. The building contained eight classrooms for grades one through eight. Each classroom had its own cloak room which always smelled like wet woolen coats and peanut butter sandwiches wrapped in wax paper and brown paper bags.

There was a storage closet under the impressive wooden stairs leading to the second floor. On the closet door hung a poster depicting a large tree from the Holy Childhood Foundation. Whenever our class scraped together five dollars worth of donations to the Foundation, we ransomed a pagan baby. First, we voted on a name for the baby. Names like Margaret Agnes were acceptable nominations, but names like Tammy Sue were not allowed. After the name had been selected, it was written on a flower sticker and the entire class would march out to the closet door where an honorary godparent would be allowed to lick the sticker and put it on the tree. By the end of the year, the tree was always resplendent with flower stickers from all the classes in school. I often wonder what happened to all those pagan babies with their Catholic names and what their former captors did with all that ransom money.

Four more classrooms, an abandoned kitchen, and an office with a desk and phone, comprised the second floor. The principal, also a teacher, was seldom in the office, and the School functioned without a secretary. When the phone rang, a student from a nearby classroom ran to answer it. The basement consisted of two lunchrooms, a furnace room, two bathrooms, and the Felice Club Room. That school, long since demolished, is such a part of me today that I could draw a blueprint or paint a picture of it. I can still smell the layers of wax that kept the hardwood floors shining. I remember all those memorized catechism lessons. I can hear the nuns' giant rosary beads click together as the sisters walked up and down rows of wooden desks with their hands modestly tucked under their scapulars, and I can see the portrait of Pope Pius XII that gazed down at us. Most of all, I can hear and feel the sharp Minnesota wind as it rattled past and beneath the gigantic windows lined up in the back of each classroom.

I remember being cold all the time. Of course, girls had to wear dresses. Tights hadn't been invented yet, and those long cotton stockings held up by garters were out of vogue. Surprisingly, St. Theodore's did not require uniforms, so we were on our own in the fashion department. Most of us wore plaid jumpers and dresses bought at the local J.C. Penney and Wards stores, ordered from catalogs, made by our mothers, or passed down by older kids.

The bottom line was this: There was no outfit from any known source that could keep a girl warm during the winter at St. Theodore's. My grandmother made me flannel petticoats and my mother bought me knee socks and cardigans, but it was a lost cause. The Franciscan nuns, all bundled up from head to toe in layers of black and brown wool, regarded sweaters as counterproductive to clear thinking. "Take that thing off and hang it in the cloak room. You don't need it in here," barked Sister Mary Teresita as she flung open windows and turned off the thermostat. Any complaint was answered with a reference to the omnipresent crucifix and a reminder that Jesus hung on a cross for three hours without complaining about heat, cold, or the thorns in his head.

Another source of discomfort was the nuns' contention that all bodily functions could and should be stifled. This practice, I am sure, is what fueled the common belief among my contemporaries that nuns never peed. We were allowed to use the bathroom only at lunch time. In theory, you could use it in an emergency if you raised your hand and asked to be excused, but those requests were handled with such an embarrassing interrogation about the nature and severity of the emergency that everyone just learned to bite the bullet.

The bathrooms were so bleak it was inconceivable that anyone would want to visit them for nefarious purposes. Located in the basement with no heat whatsoever, the girls' room contained four green wooden stalls. A student monitor reprimanded you if you had been in your stall more than your allottted thirty seconds.

After sitting on a rickety, frosty wooden toilet seat and using paper that could file off any slivers you might have picked up, you had a couple of seconds to wash hands in freezing water, wipe them with ONE paper towel and make your getaway past the Gestapo monitor. No talking was allowed, and no sins of vanity could be committed by sneaking a peek in the mirror. Most of us developed the ability to abstain from bathroom use all day, no matter how desperate we felt.

I will always be grateful to a boy named Eugene Upfall, who had the audacity to stumble up to the front of our fifth grade classroom and confront Sister Conchessa one day as she was delivering an inspired lecture on the dangers of impure thoughts. She was explaining how we should say a little prayer to St. Theresa, the Little Flower, or to the Holy Ghost, who would guide us in all matters of the flesh.

As she rhapsodized on and on, Eugene tried politely to interrupt her a couple of times. "Sister," he meekly implored, but Sister ignored him because she was off and running on her own train of thought.

I remember thinking what an idiot Eugene was for interrupting a lesson or for thinking Sister Conchessa would ever excuse him to use the bathroom, when suddenly there erupted from him an awful noise. From Eugene's mouth gushed a projectile stream of vomit headed straight for the area where Sister's bosom supposedly was located. The bravest among us ducked out of the way and watched incredulously in fear and amazement as the majority of the liquid hit the target.

Eugene was mortified. "I'm sorry, Sister," he sputtered amidst tears. In an effort to contain the mess that was headed south down her habit towards her knees, Sister daintily picked up the hem of her scapular, the tunic over her robe, and she told Eugene, in an amazingly civilized tone of voice, that he could be excused to the bathroom. A fat lot of good it was going to do anybody now!

That Eugene's accident did not trigger a chain reaction among the remaining fifth graders--some of whom had been splattered by the spray-- might have been interpreted by true believers as a modern miracle--a confirmation of our faith. What I had witnessed was so incredible I resisted the urge to surrender to my own wave of nausea so that I would be able to see whatever came next. This was such a break in routine that it was worth whatever amount of self-control it took to stick around and watch the entire event.

Still clutching her soggy and malodorous scapular, Sister Conchessa told those of us who had been in the line of fire that we could go wash as needed, and then she traipsed off to the convent across the street to change her clothes. Seizing this unprecedented moment of freedom, we all retreated to the frosty bathroom where we washed, flushed, talked, used several paper towels, and gazed into the mirror without fear of being busted.

Sister returned fifteen minutes later wearing a clean but shabby patched habit, and Eugene Upfall (his real name--no kidding!) became known at recess as Eugene Upchuck.

Although spewing vomit on his teacher and classmates was probably one of his most embarrassing moments in life, I think Eugene emerged as somewhat of a hero. He represented the culmination of a fantasy we had all entertained. "What if she won't let us go and something terrible happens?" HA! Eugene demonstrated, and now we all knew, self-control has its limits.

Eugene disproved the belief that everything of the flesh could and should be denied or suppressed. Although my friends and I discussed this incident *ad nauseam* for years to come at social get togethers and reunions, Eugene's upchuck was never again mentioned in Sister Conchessa's fifth grade classroom.

Out There on My Own
by Joan Claire Graham

I always seem to be just a little off course of where it's at. Whatever it is that everyone seems to be excited about always happens just before I get there, just after I leave, or on the next block. I'm sure to be at the airport if my ship ever comes in. I must have been one of the few 1967 college graduates who didn't have a stereo, a Beatles' album, a water pipe or a political opinion. I'm not too proud to admit that I didn't actually have a ghost of a notion about what was going on in the world.

Ten days after graduating from high school, I started college. Two years and eleven months later, at age twenty-one, I had a teaching degree with a double major. There I was--all grown up with no place to go--so I decided to start my teaching career in a small town at a private school. Private school administrators are at liberty to play fast and loose with their staff's credentials, so with a Minnesota certificate in secondary English and speech, I found myself teaching everything from religion to music, art and gym in the upper grades at Sacred Heart School in Faribault, Minnesota. I don't remember as much about the teaching as I do about my personal circumstances and my transition from college to the real world.

That first winter on my own was an incredibly mild one.   I don't think we ever had more than three inches of snow, and the warm weather enabled me to walk the eight blocks from my apartment to school. But the weather is absolutely the only warm recollection I can muster. The rest is like a bizarre dream--one of those in which the dreamer is an observer rather than a participant in a series of incongruous events, bizarre characters, and inscrutable circumstances.

The place where I lived looked quite a bit like the house Mary Tyler Moore's character lived in on her popular television show. It was a grand old Minnesota mansion converted after lifestyles changed and people no longer wanted or needed high ceilings, multiple fireplaces, formal dining rooms and miles of oak woodwork. The wealthy Victorians who built the house probably spun in their graves when the new owner, with an eye for profit rather than esthetics, chopped it up into six odd units.

My apartment ($64 per month furnished--garage included) was located across the front in what had once been the music room. My beveled glass front door was on the corner diagonal, at the edge of an open porch that ran parallel to my living room. My door opened to a little entry way with big brass coat hooks, and the living room beyond contained a fireplace with a leaded glass cupboard above, beautiful hardwood floors, and a large lace curtained window facing the porch. The residents of the other five apartments had to walk across that porch to get to their mailboxes, so I was in perfect position to observe the daily parade.

My kitchen and bathroom were stuck in at odd angles with no windows. The bedroom was just big enough for a bed and a bureau, with one window facing the street and another facing the west lawn. One of the most memorable features of that place is that it was located directly across the street from the fire station. Whenever Faribault fire fighters had a midnight run, my bedroom suddenly became kaleidoscopic with rotating red lights, and the sound of screaming sirens catapulted me right out of my dreams and into a near heart attack.   The first time it happened I thought I had died and gone to hell. This pandemonium always caused my little tuxedo cat Elizabeth to panic and retreat under the bed for a week of solitude and recuperation. About the time she would muster the courage to come out and sleep on the bed again, Faribault fire fighters would answer another middle-of-the-night call.

Another remarkable feature of that building was that I was the only so-called normal inhabitant. Mary Tyler Moore's character had lovable Rhoda and eccentric Phyllis coming and going with neighborly congeniality and amusement.   My old Victorian house was definitely not like that.   Every resident of my building had some kind of physical or mental abnormality, and to someone my age, these folks were all weird, annoying, and more than a little bit intimidating.

I remember the Conch family in apartment 6--Eugene and Shelly. I don't remember if Shelly was her real name or one I made up to go with Conch. Going through life with the name Conch would have been difficult enough, but the couple had an additional burden to bear. They had harelips and cleft palates that made their speech hard to understand, but what they lacked in diction they more than made up for in volume. Shelly and Eugene conducted screaming conversations only they could understand. You had to be a Conch to know what the issue was. They spoke or argued incessantly at unreasonably high decibel levels--about God-knows what-- on the porch, on the lawn, or in the hallways--whenever they were in the common areas together.

Upstairs in apartment 3 lived a guy with a six-inch lift on one shoe. His kitchen was above my bedroom, and he worked nights. When he came home at 1 a.m., I awakened to the sound of BOOM step, BOOM step. His poor little baby daughter had been born with an incomplete digestive system. She cried a lot because her life had been a miserable series of operations.

In the downstairs rear east apartment lived an elderly couple, the Dooleys, who spoke so loudly, I'm sure their conversations could be heard across the street at the fire station. At times, they almost drowned out the Conches. I could not understand why the Dooleys chose to holler and impatiently repeat everything three or four times rather than buy hearing aids. Though they could not hear one another across their dinner table, I could hear them at my dinner table through walls that separated us.

Though nearly deaf, the Dooleys had very sharp eyes which they used to keep track of my comings and goings. Their small talk whenever we met consisted of comments like, "YOU GOT THREE LETTERS IN THE MAIL THIS WEEK," and "WAS

THAT THE PRIEST AT YOUR DOOR YESTERDAY? MY, HE'S A NICE LOOKING MAN!" Because I had few other entertainment options and no friends my age, I used to occasionally go out to dinner with the priests of Sacred Heart Parish. I hope those outings were more exciting for the priests than they were for me.

Another co-renter was Madeline the cat lady. She was about sixty years old and had long flowing orange hair. Madeline had several cats that she talked to constantly, and she was somewhat of a horticulturist. Early that fall, she planted purple, orange and blue plastic geraniums in the window box outside my west bedroom window. They bloomed all winter, but became progressively less colorful. By spring, the afternoon sun had turned them all dirty yellow.

Eugene Conch was always trying to get on the good side of Madeline's cat, Ginger. He would call to her, but with his cleft palate, it sounded like "Here Neeynyer!" Ginger ignored Eugene, or perhaps she was fascinated by the sound of his voice. Undaunted, he would persist in trying to get her attention, repeating her name over and over--hundreds of times--in his own inimitable way. Sometimes it would go on for an hour. I once got so annoyed at having to listen to him while I was correcting papers that I opened my door and told him to stop. He looked hurt and embarrassed.

Nobody ever saw the other resident of the old mansion. He supposedly lived in the rear west apartment, right behind mine on the main floor. His name was on the mailbox, but he either didn't actually live there, was dead in his apartment, or was agoraphobic. Nobody cared one way or another.

It took about two weeks to realize that I had made a regrettable decision to work in Faribault. I felt like an outside observer--a visitor to another planet. The majority of my fellow teachers at Sacred Heart were nuns, and my social life was nearly nonexistent. All my friends were still in college having the time of their lives. I realized that small Minnesota towns held no appeal for me and started planning to move to Minneapolis at the end of the school year. If working in Faribault was what growing up was all about, I wished I hadn't been in such a hurry to get to that point.

When my children hear about the sixties, they ask me if I was a hippie or if I went to Woodstock or smoked dope or marched in peace demonstrations. I'm embarrassed to tell them that I didn't do any of those things. I missed Bob Dylan, Alan Ginsberg, LSD, Timothy Leary, The Electric Kool Aid Acid Test, the Merry Pranksters, and the Grateful Dead. If someone had held up pictures of Angela Davis, Jerry Rubin, Tom Hayden, Jack Karouac, Yoko Ono and Jimi Hendrix, I would have been hard pressed to tell you which one was which. When someone said, "Haight Ashbury," I thought they were expressing a negative opinion.

What did I do and where did I go instead? I graduated a year ahead of my classmates, got a job, and lived in a weird apartment building right out of Ripley's Believe it or Not. I walked to work in sensible shoes. I became self-sufficient. I tried to set a fine example for a bunch of Catholic school kids. I suffered in solitude, completely out of sync with my peers. My daughters can't imagine how I could have lived in that era and yet missed out on absolutely everything people of my generation were doing. I can't believe it either! How could I have been so out of step? How could I have been so square? I don't know, but I look back with amazement, reflection, and more than a little regret.

The Piano Lesson
by Joan Claire Graham

My mother's code of silence typified the Minnesota belief that some topics were strictly off limits. Like all families, we had some skeletons in our closet, and Mom believed it was her duty to make certain that those skeletons never saw the light of day. I have no doubt that she carried many secrets to her grave, but the most important one concerned the life and death of her father.

I never knew my grandfather, but I have always lived with a beautiful wedding portrait taken August 13, 1907. My grandmother's handwriting on the back identifies the six handsome and stylish members of the wedding party as herself, my grandfather, her brother, his sister, and two little flower girl cousins. Everybody in my family has a copy of this photograph, and I can not remember a time in my life when it has not been part of my home decor. I always knew that my grandfather had been a handsome man, but the only information my mother ever gave me about him was that he had been a wonderful father and that he had died rather young. When I asked about the cause of his death, she told me he had been sick. When I asked about the nature of the illness, she told me it was his heart. It was not until after her death that I started to search for details, and not until recently that I found them.

In 1905, my grandmother and three female cousins set out from their prosperous southern Minnesota homes in order to stake homestead claims in the wilds of North Dakota. Women couldn't vote, but they could own property, and so these four young women decided they needed some land along with some adventure. In order to buy a hundred and sixty acres from the government for a dollar twenty-five an acre, a homesteader had to live on and make improvements to the property for at least fourteen months and then present proof of this accomplishment to the government. The whole process took about a year and a half.

Between 1898 and 1915, approximately a quarter million people took the government up on its generous offer. But many hopeful homesteaders failed to tough it out. North Dakota's stark, cold winters and blistering hot summers, combined with buffalo stampedes, insect infestations, social isolation and hail storms that dashed hopes by ruining crops, caused thousands to abandon their dreams of becoming landowners. Seasoned farmers from Europe, seeing North Dakota homesteading as their ticket to a fresh start in a new land, were among the most likely to succeed. My grand-mother and her cousins succeeded too.

They built their cabins as near to one another as they could, dug wells, cleared twelve acres, plowed land for fire breaks, and planted gardens. They gathered buffalo and cow chips to fuel their stoves.

Four single young women had no trouble establishing a so-cial life among the railroad men, cowboys and farmers in the nearby town of Bowbells. Eventually my grandmother's charm, strength, and beauty caught the eye of Elmer Eaton, the handsome young manager of the local grain elevator. After proving her claim, Grandma paid two hundred dollars, and with the deed in her hand, she headed back to her job as a milliner in her home town of Minnesota Lake. Elmer followed her, and on August 13, 1907, the photographer snapped the picture that has always been part of my life.

The young couple returned to North Dakota, and after selling Grandma's hard-earned homestead, they bought a cozy house in town. Three years later, after my mother and her brother had been born, Elmer decided to get out of the grain elevator business and pursue a career as a salesman.

After collecting orders and deposits from buyers and borrow-ing money against the house, he bought several pianos. When these pianos arrived on the train, he loaded them onto a flat bed wagon pulled by horses. He planned to deliver the pianos, collect the balance due, and reinvest the profits.   But as the overloaded wagon undulated across the stony North Dakota terrain, disaster struck.   Nobody seems to know if it was a snake in the road that startled the lead horse or a rut that the wheel hit or merely a badly balanced load of upright pianos that simply couldn't endure the bumpy ride, but the wagon tipped over, the pianos scattered, and all but one were ruined. Elmer's family possessions were thus reduced to their clothing, a few personal possessions, and the lone surviving piano. The house had to be sold to pay for the useless shattered instruments, and the family had to move in with Elmer's parents in Iowa.

The pianos, which should have provided years of music and joy to their owners, became the symbol of Elmer's failure. His spirit, like their sounding boards, had been irreparably broken. In the years that followed, he tried to reestablish himself in the grain elevator business. Every town had one. Wheat, oats and corn that thrived on the plains were stored and weighed before being shipped to mills and markets. A man like Elmer with experience and business school training should have been able to rebound, but he never did. Frustration and failure continued to plague him, and the strain took its toll on the marriage.   After three or four false starts in as many small towns, he decided to try his luck in Canada while the family stayed in Iowa. His pain and dedication are preserved in letters he wrote to my mother and her brother.

Dear Snookums and Muggins,

I will write you a few lines tonight, as I was just thinking I had the best little boy and the best little girl in the land. I just got your letters and can see that you both are improving in your writing. I bet the teachers are glad to have such good kids come to school. I wish I was home so you could read to me. I want you fellers to take care of yourselves and not be catching colds all the time. Try to catch something that amounts to something.

Bushel baskets of kisses from,
Daddy

The children and their mother grew older, and for many years and through significant historical events and crises, the father was absent from his home. He always sent money and affectionate letters, but the family lived apart as he found short term work in one small town after another. Occasionally they would all reunite, and in 1921 a third child was born. But family unity would eventually lead to more new towns, more fresh starts, more failure, and eventual reseparation. Grandma and the kids managed without Grandpa through World War I and the deadly Spanish Influenza outbreak of 1918.

Maintaining separate residences cut into family resources, but the father mysteriously managed to scrape together money for the kids' roller skates, bicycles, dolls and-- oh yes, piano lessons. Whatever it took and wherever they went, the kids had music lessons. The sole surviving piano, an upright Packard, accompanied them from town to town. And when the kids graduated from high school, they continued their education--not at the state college located near their town but rather at MacPhail's Music Conservatory in Minneapolis. I could never understand the reason for that unlikely choice because the children were not musically gifted, and conservatory days coincided with the Great Depression. I guess they were all driven to prove to their dad that the piano was important and was being put to the best possible use.

Mom's brother eventually became a music teacher, and Grandpa and Grandma reunited and moved to Adrian, a small town in southwestern Minnesota where Elmer worked for the local grain elevator. Toward the end of his second year, he was fired. Old timers claim there was a scandal involving embezzlement. Rumors of that kind generally have some basis in fact.

On the morning of June 12, 1939, Elmer rose early, wrote a note, and left the house. A few hours later, his body was found in the river. A farmer who owned the land the river flowed through reported seeing a solitary man walk across the field early that morning. A newspaper article described his death.

Following a two or three month period of ill health and business worries, which became unbearable, he chose to lay down his burdens and passed this life on Monday at the age of 61. To the grief stricken family he left a message that explained it all.

My grandfather's life and death were then diminished by a code of silence which kept his life story secret from his grandchildren. Nearly sixty years later when I began to search for his story, I found the small town librarian to be a bit of a detective. Many mysteries shrouded my grandfather's demise, and some have still not been solved. I doubt that the facts of his life could have been any worse than those I was forced to imagine.

In violation of state law, no death certificate was filed in the county where he died. No death certificate was filed in the county where he was buried. Nobody can or will tell me what was said in that letter that reportedly explained it all. Because the death certificate was not handled correctly and because of the embezzlement rumors, I have a feeling that there may have been foul play, and that foul play may have followed years of illegal business dealings.

This feeling was reinforced by a couple of facts. First, following the death of her husband, my grandmother moved across the state to Mankato, a town where she had never lived before. She completed this move within a month of my grandfather's death, which suggests that she fled in shame. Second, the librarian eventually found the death certificate misfiled in St. Paul with the state health department. Using information from the attached report, she located the place in the river where the body was found. After researching precipitation and spring run-off from melting snow, she concluded, "Not even a rabbit could have drowned in the Kanaranzi River in 1939."

Sixty years after the death of my grandfather, I visited the town, the river, and the librarian. We hopped into her pickup and stood at the banks of the so-called river, a little rocky stream that meanders through the wheat fields in view of the town's grain elevator. The late afternoon sun twinkled on the slowly moving water, which was about two feet deep. It would have been nearly impossible for an adult to willingly hold himself under until he was drowned. Was he murdered and then thrown in among the rocks? Did he take poison before going into the river? Did the police participate in a conspiracy? If there was an investigation at the time, the tracks of it were skillfully covered. No record exists today, unless it too was misfiled.

Somebody once knew more than I know now, but why was everything kept secret? Why did everyone discount my grandfather's existence by refusing to talk about either his life or his death? Was the shame he brought unbearable? Was he a bad man? Did he commit unspeakable crimes? Did he deserve to be shut out of all our lives?

My mother and grandmother lived for more than thirty years after my grandfather's tragic death, strictly observing their code of silence. It is apparent now that the heart trouble my mother vaguely described as the cause of her father's death was emotional rather than physical.

My ninety-three year old uncle, the last of Elmer's children, recently told me as much as I know. An abandoned sign reading "Piano Lessons" is propped up against his garage, but for decades, hundreds of children trooped through his living room for their weekly lessons on his Steinway grand. I often wonder about all the other pianos that have been part of our lives. My mother bought one for me at a time when she had little money for anything else, and my sister, brother and I trudged off to weekly lessons where we learned to bang out "Fur Elise" and "The Spinner's Song." My cousins grew up with piano lessons, and after I graduated from college and started to teach, my grandmother gave me money for a down payment on a little Wurlitzer spinet. It was as if the music filled the void left by the missing words.

I don't know if I will continue to look for the complete story. Adrian old-timers could tell me more than I already know, as I have discovered that there is no such thing as a secret. We are always leaving tracks, even when we think otherwise. If I find the missing pieces of my puzzle, it will not be for the sake of exploiting the crimes of the grandfather I never knew, but rather to understand him and bring closure. He is a part of me and my children. He did his best. He deserves to be remembered.

Family Reunion
by Joan Claire Graham

Early Minnesota families tended to be large. Whether to keep warm on winter nights or to provide farmers with enough sons to till the earth, our grandparents tended to produce large numbers of offspring. As these children grew older, established lives away from the farm, and produced progeny of their own, someone decided it would do everyone a lot of good to participate in a yearly ritual known as the family reunion.

Both my parents' families went along with this plan. I enjoyed the Graham get-togethers, but the Eatons were enigmatic and inscrutable, and their reunions were torturous ordeals.

The Grahams, consisting of two Irish grandparents, seven children, and eighteen grandchildren, got together every summer at Uncle Bob's farm in Henderson. The farm kids were a fun-loving and rowdy bunch who found joy in teaching their city cousins how to do things we had never imagined possible--like rock an outhouse while someone was inside or hypnotize a chicken. The adults, who left the kids alone, pitched horseshoes, told stories, laughed uproariously, argued, spread out the feast, and consumed copious amounts of food and beer. Since everyone dressed casually for a day on the farm and acted without formality, restraint or pretense, a Graham reunion required very little preparation or fanfare. However, because of excess food, drink, and fun, participants required several days to recuperate.

The Eaton reunions were completely different. My grandmother, who had eleven siblings, married a man with eight. The Eatons were a stuffy and proper bunch of English Episcopalians whose idea of a good time would have elicited ridicule from the Grahams. Perhaps they practiced restraint in order to guard the secret of my grandfather's suicide, or maybe they were just naturally stuffy and brittle. For whatever reason, they never appeared to have any fun.

Dressed in their Sunday best, car loads of Eatons gathered each August in the pavilion of a picnic park in Rochester. Nobody in the family lived in Rochester, but this location was chosen because it was a geographical compromise that most family members could reach after approximately the same amount of driving. The weather gods always sent temperatures soaring into triple digits to further ensure that attendees would be as miserable as possible. Men and women, soaked in sweat, engaged in polite conversation before someone decided to break the spell by shooing flies away and urging us to chow down before the food turned bad. After cleaning up the mess, waving farewell and climbing back into hot cars, everyone drove back to wherever they had come from.

I never understood who anybody in the Eaton clan was, nor did I know how they knew me or why they would care. My mother always treated the event like a Holy Day of Obligation so I had no choice about attending. I suppose that since the older people knew who the kids were, they figured the kids must also know the adults. Unfortunately, it doesn't automatically work that way.

Forty years after these dreaded assemblies, when I wrote a book about my mother's family, I finally put some pieces together and learned how the Eatons at those reunions were related to me. I missed out by not knowing, caring, or talking to the Eatons. Not only did they have interesting lives and stories, but some of them would have been able to tell me about my grandfather.

Uncle Lonnie, my grandfather's brother, was the ancient tiny, wizened man I watched trying to scoop melted vanilla ice cream from a Dixie Cup with a shaking flat wooden spoon one sweltering day in Rochester. While I was researching the book, I learned that Lonnie weighed less than three pounds at birth. The family kept the tiny baby in an incubator fashioned from a shoe box set on the oven door, and the midwife slipped her wedding ring around his wrist. Always diminutive, he grew up and played the fiddle. What an interesting guy he must have been! Was he the inspiration behind my mother's violin lessons?

And how about those other strangers? Why didn't anybody introduce us or encourage the old to share family stories with the young? What did they know? Could his brothers and sisters have told me about my grandfather if I had known what or whom to ask? Did I look like him or remind anybody of him? Did I inherit my writing talent from the man who wrote eloquent letters to his children? And what about the depression that drove him to suicide at age sixty-one? Did he seek help? Was he a melancholy child? Did he drop any clues?

I don't think the Eaton reunions would have ever held a candle to the rollicking good times enjoyed by the Grahams, but in retrospect, I don't think they had to have been as insufferable as they were. If time travel were possible, and if there were no embargoes placed on conversation topics, I'd like to get all dolled up in my best cotton dress and sandals, endure the heat, put fresh batteries in my tape recorder, and go back for one more family reunion in that Rochester pavilion.

But What Will They *Call* Him?
by Joan Claire Graham

Call it a tradition or a tendency or a way of making your people feel like they're your people, but one thing Minnesotans do better than people from other parts of the country is rename their people. Just like everyone else in the world, Minnesotans are given names at birth. These names are written on birth and death certificates and in telephone directories, but aside from those formal listings, many Minnesotans are known in social and business circles by their nicknames. My Minnesotans didn't ever use the word nickname but preferred to use the word "call." When a baby's name was announced, people would wonder, "Yes, but what will they *call* him?"

Translated, this phrase means, "His name is Charles, but what are they going to *call* him?" It would not suffice to simply call him Charles because that would be too simple. His name needs to be customized so that our Charles will be unique and will therefore receive full initiation into the tribe. Re-namers will cast aside obvious diminutive forms like Charlie or Chuck and end up calling this little guy something like Goober or Bean. And most surprisingly, many folks, including the renamed person, will go along with casting aside a perfectly normal name in favor of this new name for years--possibly for life.

My parents knew folks in Albert Lea who were known throughout the community as Duckie, Fizz, Frowzie, Tish, Shanty, Pinkie, Dinky and Babe. A guy named Sweat Olson cut my hair, and Buzz Knutson sold shoes. I went to school with kids who signed their names Ditto, Doc, Mouse, Chickie, Kitty, Dutch, Swede, Sternwheel, Cokie, Sis, Bub, Sonny, Ky, Muffy, Tootie, Punk, Spuds, Weiner and Chrome Dome. My brother went to the prom with a girl called Cookie and ran around with a guy who ordered his graduation cards printed with the name Stud. My dad had a cousin everyone called Shag and a brother called Buck, and we had a paper boy called Red. Of course, those were not their real names, but they were what people *called* them and what they preferred to be *called.*

Although being called something other than your given name was common in Albert Lea, it was mandatory in Minnesota Lake, a few miles west. The tiny town was the world capital of nick-names. Perhaps natives figured it might make the town appear bigger if they gave each person two names. As a kid, I was in a constant state of confusion. My grandmother's family of twelve kids had produced a batch of aunts, uncles and cousins who were related to me, but I never knew who any of them were because everybody had at least two names, some for family use and others for social use, and none of the names made any sense.

My family spent every Memorial Day of my wonder years in Minnesota Lake with the maternal cousins, visiting the living and putting geraniums on the graves of the dead. Not even the names on the graves made any sense because they didn't match the names people talked about. My grandma's cousin Anne, whom everyone called Ben, was the matriarch of a gaggle of cousins of various degrees--first, second, once and twice removed. I never under-stood who was which or who anyone was ever talking about.

In 1993, I brought along my journal when I interviewed my Aunt Alexia "Lex" "Joan" and her husband Orville "John" "Johnny" Klosterman in Albert Lea. At least they went by di-minutive forms of their first or middle names, which makes some sense. We went over to Hy-Vee to catch the $1.49 three-course breakfast and talk about family history. They talked and I wrote. I already knew a small amount of what they told me, but they cracked the code and erased most of my confusion about family names that had clouded my brain for forty years.

My grandmother's name was Clara, but everyone in the fam-ily called her Sal or Sally. She signed her paintings Sally Bye but encouraged everyone to name their daughters Clara, a name she professed to love. Everyone called her brother Steven "Max," her sister Mary, "Cherry," and her brother Edward, "Sike." So when Steven, Max, Mary, Cherry, Clara, Sally, Edward and Sike all showed up for lunch, they actually only needed four teacups.

Ben's sons, Dorman and George, were known as Blip and Yaatz. They would regale us with tales of their uncles Herman and William, a.k.a. Slugger and Riley. I don't know if Slugger was a baseball player or a boxer. He may have been neither. Nobody ever explained the name's origin. Friends and relatives called my Uncle Albert "Zilch" but offered no explanation.

The name that used to catch my ear and amuse me with its musical and whimsical lilt was Uncle Oompie. Surely, I thought, no priest ever poured water over a baby's head and said, "I baptize thee in the name of Oompie." There had to have been another name, a saint's name. The mystery was solved that morning at Hy-Vee when the identity of Oompie was revealed as Paul, brother of Anne, a.k.a. Ben. Why would someone named Paul allow people to call him Oompie? I could understand if his original name was worse than Oompie but can't for the life of me come up with a name I'd be willing to give up in favor of Oompie.

Mother's cousin, Marie, had an interesting setup. Marie and her husband Ralph were bartenders. Everybody in Minnesota Lake called Marie "Charlie" and Ralph "Jerry." Another cousin named Jerry was somehow allowed to use his real name, even though it duplicated the name someone else in the family was *called*, even though that other person's real name was Ralph.

My mom, Aquinata, preferred to be called Cookie. She had always hated her unusual name, so when she moved to Albert Lea, her friends suggested Cookie as an alternative to Cracker, which they associated with Graham. I think she enjoyed being a Cookie after so many years of having to spell and explain Aquinata. It also had a kind of girlish glamor, a reminder of her youthful days on the stage. Imagine how pleased she was when my brother found a prom date who was also called Cookie.

When I was born, friends and relatives tried to call me by another name, but I refused to accept the honor. They tried Jodie and Sis, and my brother had a go at Mudslinger. I outwitted them when I learned that if I turned a deaf ear when people called me those names, the callers would eventually get frustrated and try to get my attention by using my given name. If Sweat Olson had figured out that trick, he would have been known by his beauty salon customers as DeWitt. That's the name I read on his license posted in his shop.

When I named my daughters Jennifer and Susannah, the first question everyone asked was, "But what are you going to *call* them?" We called them Jenny and Susie until they moved to California where spokespeople for the politically correct, who were obviously not in tune with Minnesota culture, led us all to believe that nicknames and diminutive name forms suggested a compromise or denial of one's heritage. They dropped the diminutives and went by their full names in California. Jennifer moved back to Minnesota as an adult, however, and became Jen in about fifteen minutes. Susannah lives in New York where her name remains intact.

I suppose people from other places use nicknames too. I don't think Minnesotans of my memories held the patent on their invention of new names, but they certainly took their work seriously and did their work well. The invented names suggested good humor and camaraderie, and they added something special to our social lives. Their wide acceptance helped create a social bond. Those who were called something felt akin to those who did the calling, and common acceptance of *calling* perpetuated this practice..... or this tradition...... or whatever you want to *call* it.

Radio Fan
by Joan Claire Graham

Before "I Love Lucy" and "The $64,000 Question" turned Americans into television addicts, radio played a vital role in our small town lives. We woke up to hear Don McNeill marching around the table at his Breakfast Cub and stayed tuned to hear Paul Harvey intone the news at noon. Afternoon soap opera commercials informed us that Halo is the shampoo that glorifies your hair and Oxydol beats the sun for getting clothes brighter. Arthur Godfrey said, "How ah ya," fired Julius LaRosa, and strummed his ukulele, and Art Linkletter proved repeatedly that kids say the darndest things. On Saturday morning, Big John and Sparky announced, "No school today!" and introduced kids to the world of literature and music with recorded books and stories like *Horton Hatches the Egg* and *Rusty in Orchestraville.*

Although the national shows were wonderful, local programming provided balance and reflected the values of our community. In fact, local radio helped create our southern Minnesota community. Right after The Breakfast Club signed off, Albert Lea's own Marie Prosser signed on to inform locals about all events of interest in the city. When Marie ran out of school plays and garden club meetings to discuss, she read recipes. We all felt we knew Marie. Don Franz, hometown guy whose hobby was collecting vintage jazz recordings, aired tunes from his personal collection every Sunday night and in two decades never played the same record twice.

At noon, local livestock quotations informed farmers of market prices. Three cow moos, each one louder and more impatient than the last, provided a unique theme song that heralded the livestock quotations. The prices seemed like important information for residents of a packing house town, even though radio listeners and a few announcers didn't understand what those words and numbers actually meant.

One rookie announcer amused townsfolk when he encountered the unfamiliar word "ewes" on-air while reading the livestock update. The poor guy stopped for a second, and then, remembering that the show must go on, replaced dead air, took the plunge, and pronounced "ee-wees" to listeners who still recall his blunder.

The semi-professional Albert Lea Packers of the Southern Minne League packed baseball fans into the stands at Hayek Field a couple of times a week all summer. Although the park was only a few blocks from our house, we plugged the radio to an extension cord and sat out on the front porch eating popcorn and listening to Jimmy Delmont describe plays and strategy of Shanty Dolan, Babe Jensen and the Marquardt brothers, Rollie and Del. When the crowd cheered a play over at the park, we could hear the sound both on the radio and over the breeze that blew through towering elms.

KATE radio station of Albert Lea was headquartered above a store on South Broadway, but they frequently set up remote operations. They broadcast band concerts from the Fountain Lake band shell and chatted with visitors at the Freeborn County Fair. During one summer, a DJ took requests from customers and spun records in a local music store. KATE broadcast high school basketball games and aired weekly services from the First Lutheran Church.

The strangest KATE show I can remember was the nightly broadcast of the rosary during Lent. My dad took me up the steep stairs of KATE a few times where I knelt on the floor and intoned Hail Marys with a large group of fellow radio star hopefuls. Friends told me a stranger story from nearby Winona where radio station KWNO tested listeners' imaginations by broadcasting Fourth of July fireworks. Shall we watch the fireworks this year? Heck no. Why go down by the lake and get eaten by mosquitoes when you can just as well turn on the radio and enjoy the colorful spectacle from the comfort of your living room? Local radio fans accepted and appreciated whatever their radio stations put on the air.

My most exciting personal experience with local radio came one summer evening in the early fifties. Mom started listening to an evening show that awarded prizes to lucky listeners who sent in postcards and were able to answer a question when their postcard got picked out of a barrel. Mom had won a couple of prizes in drawings, and she must have figured she was on a roll. She sent in a postcard with her name and phone number, and as an afterthought, just for the heck of it, sent in one for her sister Lex, who lived across town.

The game, which came on after supper, was sponsored by the local Ford dealership. After chatting with the Ford manager about cars he had to sell, the announcer picked a postcard and called a player. The Ford company posted a quote in their showroom, which encouraged potential prize winners and car buyers to stop by, take a look at the merchandise, and learn the quote so they could win a prize. If a contestant didn't know the quote or wasn't home, the radio host upped the ante for the following night by adding another prize.

My mother never drove a car, so her visits to the Ford showroom were made strictly for the purpose of winning the contest. Each night as the game started, she sat by the radio and the phone, clutching a paper on which she'd written the current quote.

This particular week's quote was, "The bigger they are, the harder they fall." For the last two nights, the radio host had called people who hadn't known the answer, so in addition to the twelve-inch, three-speed, electric oscillating fan and the haircut from Ray's Barber Shop, the local Coca Cola bottling company had added a case of Coke to the prize package. The stakes, as well as the tension, were high.

Trying to fill dead air, the announcer called out the numbers he was dialing, 7-3-2-3. Oh my gosh, that was Lex's number, and Mom knew that Lex did not know, "The bigger they are, the harder they fall." Lex never even listened to this show.

"Hello," I heard my Uncle Johnny say over the radio. He sounded different over the airwaves.

"Hello, Mr.......ah, is it Klosterman?"

"Yes, that's right," said my Uncle Johnny. We could hear his kids screaming in the background. It was suppertime, and they screamed a lot. Lex was probably trying to shush them and had no idea who Johnny was talking to on the phone.

The announcer tried to make the show interesting with a little small talk. "This is Don Franz from radio station KATE. How are you this evening, Mr. Klosterman?

Not waiting to hear how he was, my mother started thinking and scheming fast. She wanted to win those prizes, and she wanted to win them badly. Grabbing the slim Albert Lea phone book, she riffled through pages and found the number of the people who lived next door to Lex and Johnny. Luckily, their name was Register. There was only one family with that name in Albert Lea so Mom didn't have to wade through a sea of Johnsons or Andersons to find the right people. Mom was squealing and shrieking and jumping up and down as she dialed Gordy Register's phone. Luckily, the Registers did not share a party line with the Klostermans; otherwise Mom would have gotten a busy signal and the story would end here.

One of the Register daughters, I think it was Joanne, picked up the phone and was shocked and confused to hear my mother, whom she didn't know very well, shrieking, "Lex, Lex, the radio show, run and tell Lex, 'The bigger they are, the harder they fall'."

"What??" asked the frightened child. "Who is this? What are you talking about?"

Meanwhile, back at the radio, Don Franz was asking my uncle about his job. Just like everyone else in town, Johnny worked at the meat packing plant so that was a short and uninteresting line of questioning.

Back at the phone, my mom was still shrieking and getting nowhere with poor, confused Joanne Register. "Don't ask any questions!! Just run next door and tell Lex, 'The bigger they are, the harder they fall'!!"

"Who are you? Why are you yelling? Who is Lex?"

Mom's sister's name was Alexia, but she hated the name and preferred to be called by her middle name Joan. Everyone outside the family called her Joan and knew nothing of Lex or Alexia.

"Lex! Alexia! Joan! The radio show is calling! 'The bigger they are, the harder they fall'!"

Over the radio, I heard my uncle telling Don Franz that he lived on Route 1 and that his children were a boy and a girl, aged three and one.

"Radio show? Calling who? What radio show? Who are you? Why are you calling me? What are you saying?" asked the confused Register child. My mother's anxiety was mounting.

"Listen!" my mom finally articulated, "The radio show is calling! Run next door and tell Lex-Alexia-Alexia-I mean JOAN--"THE BIGGER THEY ARE, THE HARDER THEY FALL!' Don't ask what it means. Just run as fast as you can, tell her what I just said, and don't ask any more questions!" There must have been something in her demeanor that triggered blind compliance in the dazed and confused child.

Riveted to the radio, we heard Uncle Johnny start to explain to Don Franz that he wasn't a regular listener and didn't know tonight's quote. But suddenly in the background, we heard a young female voice scream, "Lux Radio Theatre is calling! Election! Election! JOAN! 'The bigger they are, the harder they fall'!"

"I think I hear one of your children-- or possibly your wife--saying something in the background," coaxed the radio announcer. "It sounds like she might have tonight's answer after all."

We all breathed sighs of relief and then cheered jubilantly as the Klostermans won the radio jackpot, thanks to Mom's quick thinking. Johnny went down to Ray's Barber shop the next day for his free haircut, and Lex asked us over to enjoy a bottle of Coke and share their bounty. Since they already had a twelve-inch, oscillating electric fan, and since they would have never won the contest without mother's help, the Klostermans decided to give us their old fan. Even though it was July in Minnesota, who needed the luxury of two fans? We accepted it with pleasure, used it for years, and always called it our radio fan.

C'mon, C'mon, C'mon
by Joan Claire Graham

My dad was born on a farm, where getting an early start was the way people got chores done. Farmers rose before dawn and worked either until the work was done, daylight was gone, or they could work no longer. The early start was a necessity back on the farm, but it was a habit Dad could never break after he moved to town. His quickness out of the gate would not have affected the rest of the family if his behavior hadn't gotten out of hand.

As Dad grew older, the wisdom and common sense he learned as a young farm lad developed into a disorder. Punctuality, which could have been his virtue, turned and twisted its way into an obsessive compulsive behavior that ruled our lives and drove us crazy.

After leaving the farm, he moved to Albert Lea and worked at Wilson's Meat Packing Plant, where work began at 6 a.m. Since the plant was over a mile from our house, Dad rose at 4:30 so he could eat a hearty breakfast and be in his car by 5:30. On the busiest traffic day, it couldn't have taken more than three minutes to drive to the plant through abandoned predawn streets, so in thirty years, Dad gave Wilson's thousands of extra hours.

If Dad's compulsion to be early had been limited to his work, we would have smiled and tolerated it. However, it spilled over into all aspects of our lives and got worse as the man grew older.

If church started at 8:00, we had to be in the car ready to go by 7:30, even though St. Theodore's Church was only ten blocks from our house. He had an irritating habit of getting everyone agitated by waving two fingers as if to round us up and uttering the phrase, "C'mon, c'mon, c'mon." If we didn't hop right to it, he'd breathe a sharp breath through his teeth, get a look on his face like he'd just smelled ammonia, and repeat the gesture and sound until he had us in a state of panic. We'd fly around the house, find our hats and gloves and pile into the Ford."

Dad never actually drove to the church, however. He stopped two blocks short of the place and avoided church parking lot congestion by parking two blocks up Clark Street. Even if it was below zero and we females begged to be dropped off at the church door to avoid freezing our exposed limbs, Dad refused to take the extra minute to accommodate us. He said he had to save time so he'd park short of the church and make us run the last two blocks.

Arriving early allowed Dad to sit in his favorite pew at the back of the church. When the priest uttered the last "Go in peace," Dad would bolt out the door and dash back to his car, hop in and be home before his fellow worshipers had even realized Mass had ended. He enjoyed being the first one home more than he enjoyed attending Mass.

Dad's hurry-up compulsion embarrassed me whenever it affected non family members. One hot summer afternoon, my friend Carol Adair rode along with us when Dad had to buy something in Mankato. The initial plan was that he'd transact his business and then we'd all visit my grandma. Mankato was an hour's drive from Albert Lea, so we figured we might as well stop in and see Grandma Sal while we were in her town. She always had a supply of cookies and seemed to enjoy drop-in visits.

Spotting a carnival with rides set up in a Mankato super market lot near the edge of town, we begged to be dropped off while Dad spoke to a guy who was selling a car part. We girls thought we'd have a half hour to spend our hard-earned babysitting money at the carnival before continuing on to visit Sal.

Since we only had a dollar between us, Carol and I took a minute to choose how we'd spend it. A dollar got us two rides, the Tilt-a-Whirl and the Ferris Wheel. Lines were short so we hopped right on the Tilt-a-Whirl for three minutes of excitement. But Ferris Wheels take a while to load, so we had to make a few stops to fill all the seats. As we enjoyed the thrill of stopping near the top, we bravely rocked our seat and admired the Mankato vista.

Shattering our fun, amidst squeals and carnival music, we suddenly heard a car honking repeatedly. Searching for the source of the noise far below, we caught sight of Dad's car. Amazingly, from way down there, his impatient gaze met my inquiring eyes just as the wheel advanced to its apex and stopped.

There I was, stopped at the top of the Ferris wheel, forty feet up. He caught my eye, honked his horn some more, made that irritating gesture with his two fingers, and mouthed the words, "C'mon, c'mon, c'mon." I felt I had no choice but to leap out of the ride, but Carol managed to restrain me. Five minutes later, when a tattooed carnie unloaded us, Carol and I ran to the car and hopped in. Dad announced that because we had wasted so much of his time, we would not be able to complete our itinerary and visit Grandma.

My childhood memories are cluttered with incomplete itineraries. We'd plan to spend a week's vacation at a northern Minnesota lake cabin. After making reservations, we'd busily sew new shorts, buy cans of mosquito spray from the Fuller brush man, pack the cooler, cancel the mail and newspaper delivery, and organize our fishing poles. We'd pile into the Ford before dawn so we could miss Minneapolis rush-hour and show up for cabin check-in at the lake before last week's renters had even checked out.

After about two days of swimming and fishing, Dad would start to squirm. By the third day, he'd be in a full blown state of agitation. He'd tell us he had to get home to go to the bank, get a haircut, or mow the lawn. Heck, we'd seen all there was to see at the lake anyway, so we might as well go home, "C'mon, c'mon, c'mon." No amount of begging could dissuade him, so we'd sadly pack up and head home, leaving the rented cabin sitting empty for half a week.

One time, he cut the vacation especially short when he got as far as Minneapolis, spotted what he perceived might have been a rain cloud, turned around, and drove home. If he was supposed to pick me up at a friend's house, he'd show up an hour early.   If he went to a movie or a concert, he'd be at the theatre before the ushers opened the doors. The anger or inconvenience caused by arriving too early did nothing to prevent him from repeating the same behavior time and time again.

After I grew up and moved to Robbinsdale, Dad's compulsion continued to plague me. He'd try to stay in touch by phoning or visiting. When he'd call, he'd say, "Hi, how are you doing? Fine? How are the kids? Good? Well, I'd better go. Good-bye." I used to jokingly paraphrase his phone calls with, "Hi, I just called so that I could hang up."

Dad's visits were worse than the phone calls. He'd plan to come, arrive early, and leave as soon as possible. One time he drove two hours, arrived an hour early, and stayed fifteen minutes. One of my kids was in the bathroom and missed seeing him entirely.

One time, I managed to round up a batch of relatives to celebrate the June birthday of my oldest daughter. My dad and his second wife agreed to bring the Klostermans, Johnny and Lex. My Uncle Al and his family as well as my brother and his family lived in the Minneapolis area so they all planned to join us for a pot luck supper. To accommodate those who had to drive a hundred miles home down I35, I told everyone to come at 5:00.

Since it was one of the first days of summer vacation, I slept late, arose at 9, and made a list while taking my morning hit of caffeine: 1 Shower, 2. Bathe the kids, 3. Clean house, 4. Go to butcher, 5. Pick up the cake, 6. Wash clothes. 7. Clean the cat box. No problem, seven tasks in eight hours, I thought as I surveyed a sea of clutter. The kids would have to pitch in, but everything should be in shape by late afternoon. As I made this pronouncement, the doorbell rang. Gathering my pink robe around me, I stumbled over two cats and a pair of roller skates and pulled open the back door. There, holding a birthday present, a pot of baked beans, and a bag of chips, stood my dad, his wife, and the Klostermans.

My heart stopped. "You're early!" I exclaimed. It was bad enough that they had shown up seven hours early, but they had caught me at my worst. Since the older generation did not share my tolerance for clutter, I was humiliated and angry. The visitors looked confused as I thrust into their hands a twenty dollar bill and driving directions to the butcher and the baker.

As their car pulled out of the driveway, I ran to the basement and dumped all the dirty laundry onto the floor. Grabbing the empty clothes baskets, I bolted back up the stairs two at a time, rushed to the living room, and loaded the baskets with all the junk that had cluttered the living room, dining room, and kitchen. Everything from old Tribunes to Fisher Price stoves went into the baskets and down to the basement.

Having no time to put things away properly, I elected to get them out from under foot. I dumped the first loads on the floor next to the dirty laundry and raced upstairs for more. In ten minutes, the upstairs looked orderly, but the basement looked like a war zone. I hopped into the shower, got the kids up and washed, and decided the laundry and the cat box would just have to wait till tomorrow. I didn't actually know if I could even find the dirty laundry amidst all that junk, but I could easily follow my nose to the dirty cat box. Never mind, toss the cats into the basement and shut the door. Tomorrow I'll clean. Today I have guests to entertain.

Shortly before 10, my dad, his wife and the Klostermans reappeared with the chicken and the birthday cake. They oohed and aahed and expressed surprise when they saw the clean house miracle I'd managed to pull off. I modestly accepted credit while I racked my brain for a clue as to what I would do with them for seven hours until the others arrived.

If it hadn't been for the Klostermans, my dad would have left by noon, missing the birthday party and the other relatives completely. But Johnny had driven his car, and he refused to buckle to my dad's insistence to "C'mon, c'mon, c'mon." Johnny was impervious to the frenzy that utterance provoked in the rest of us.

Lex drew me aside and confided that Dad had routed her and Johnny out of bed at dawn, telling them the party started at noon. I assured her that since it was a week day, it was highly unlikely that members of my generation, most of whom had jobs, would attend any social events until at least 5 p.m. She apologized profusely. I knew it was going to be a difficult day.

Around 3:30, I oven-fried the chicken, and by 5 p.m., cousins, uncles, aunts and siblings started to arrive with birthday presents, Jello molds, bars and home made rolls. Sunny skies were beginning to cloud over, and sensing my dad's growing agitation, I suggested we eat immediately so that those who needed to drive could get home before dark. The situation grew worse, however. As we devoured piles of potato salad from plastic plates, but before we could toast the birthday girl, the still June air was pierced by the wail that fills every Minnesotan with dread--the emergency civil defense siren.

In denial, I thought, "It's the first Wednesday of the month. It's noon. They always test the sirens.......oh, oh. It's not Wednesday, it's not noon, and it's the middle of the month." Turning on the radio, I heard the words I hoped I might never hear. No, the Russians were not attacking Robbinsdale; it was far worse than a nuclear attack. A tornado was headed straight for our house some time within the next twenty minutes. We had no choice. I was doomed. The civil defense team instructed us to seek shelter in the southwest corner of--oh no--the basement. This was stacking up to be one of the worst days of my life.

Two formerly lonely cats swarmed through a grove of ankles as twelve adults and four kids picked their way down the cluttered basement steps. Even before they reached the bottom, the smell of the litter box told all my relatives that this was no ordinary trip to the basement. This was gross beyond their wildest expectations. The condition of this basement showed what kind of a person I really was.

My dad didn't even try to camouflage his disgust as he stepped over piles of toys and dirty underwear. There was nowhere to sit. Junk was everywhere. Sixteen people and two cats bit the bullet, tried to breathe, stood close together, and listened for a reprieve on the radio.

A half hour later, when the weather service sounded the "all-clear" signal, I finally heard the words I knew I'd hear.

"C'mon, c'mon, c'mon. Let's get going. Let's hit the road before the weather gets worse." For the first time in my life, those words were music to my ears.

Mother's Good Bavarian China
by Joan Claire Graham

I remember a bleak winter morning in the late forties when Mother's Good Bavarian China arrived amidst a flurry of excitement. Delivery men hauled into our Minnesota living room two crates from the Johann Seltmann Company of Vohenstrauss. The crates appeared to be filled with excelsior, but nestled in packing material that to my three-year-old eyes looked like shredded bird nests, were precious fine china plates and teacups decorated with pink rosebuds, blue daisies, and gold trim. My mother cautioned me not to touch anything as she carefully unpacked and inventoried the shipment and then lovingly bathed and arranged her treasures on a high shelf. Everything appeared to be perfect about what Mother immediately christened her Good Bavarian China.

The paradoxical compulsion to own and maintain beautiful but impractical imported dinnerware was buried with my mother and I suspect with many other women of her generation. Mother survived the Great Depression with her "waste not, want not" philosophy intact, but she maintained this one luxury in her otherwise drab life.

Throughout her life, she darned socks, made pillow cases and dresses from cotton flour sacks, saved and reused zippers and buttons from worn-out clothing, and made me a coat carefully cut from a pair of my dad's old trousers. She could feed her family for two days with a pot full of soup made from a bone, some barley and a few carrots, and she spent sweltering August days boiling bell jars filled with tomatoes to nurture her family until next summer's crops ripened. She replaced heels and soles of shoes until her toes peeked out from holes in the uppers, and she rotated everyone's top bed sheet to the bottom every week and hung laundered bottom sheets on the line every Monday. She would have won the Mrs. Frugality contest if there had been such a thing, if it had not been for her solitary luxury --a high cupboard filled with Good Bavarian China.

Mother deferred ownership of her Good Bavarian China until after World War II because shipment had been impossible during war years. Mother had squirreled away inherited money with hope that she would someday be able to defy common sense and purchase her own set of Good Bavarian China. In the prosperous aftermath of the war, she finally treated herself to this guilty pleasure. My father certainly did not underwrite such frivolity, and it is amazing that she overrode his opposition to her one indulgence.

After unpacking her exquisite dishes, Mother began to make plans for their initial use. "I'll save them for Christmas dinner," she announced. Since it was February, that gave her plenty of time to crochet a fine tablecloth, sew and embroider some linen napkins, and do all that was needed to set the perfect table. When the holiday season approached, however, she suffered a setback after she tallied her guest list. She planned to host her mother, her sister and brother-in- law, her bachelor brother, and a fellow who rented our fourth bedroom. Add the four of us, and that brought the number of diners to nine. There were only eight place settings of Good Bavarian China so rather than create a third world war by giving someone a mismatched plate, she decided she'd better save the Good Bavarian China for a more mathematically appropriate occasion.

"Next Christmas," she figured, "my mother will have the whole gang at her house, so I'll have to wait two years." Two years later, the roomer had moved out, but Mom's brother had married and her sister had adopted two kids. Even though the kids were technically too young to eat off Good Bavarian China, the new cast of characters forced Mother to defer the China inauguration to the following spring, when my brother would make his First Holy Communion.

Spring arrived, and as the Holy Communicants prepared for their big day, Mom lovingly washed and prepared her Good Bavarian China. But as luck would have it, my brother's godparents announced their plans to attend the big event, thus throwing the family once again into a Good Bavarian China shortage.

"I wish I would have ordered a service for twelve," she lamented. Of all things I remember her saying, I remember her saying that phrase most often.

Mother postponed the debut of her Good Bavarian China time and time again. Either there weren't enough dishes, or else the occasion just didn't cut the mustard and warrant the use of such good china. My brother's Confirmation, my First Holy Communion, my Confirmation, my sister's Baptism, her First Holy Communion and Confirmation, countless Christmas dinners, graduation feasts, baby and wedding showers came and went, but the dishes, the good china, remained unused in the high cupboard.

Eventually, the dishes took on a life of their own and came to represent hopes and dreams that hadn't panned out. As she lay dying of cancer in 1972, Mother gave me her Good Bavarian China, which I accepted with a heavy heart.

I packed my inheritance in shredded newspaper for safe transport and brought the dishes to my home. For twenty-seven years, I admired their pink roses, blue daisies, and gold trim displayed behind a glass curio door. The idea of using the dishes always triggered a wave of melancholy. I missed my mom, and I missed her dreams of the grandest, most perfect family dinner that never was. I missed her eternal hope that a perfect occasion befitting the use of her Good Bavarian China would ever occur.

Facing the end of the millennium, I decided to break the spell. I washed dust off the plates, polished the cups, ironed a fine table cloth and set a beautiful table.

Three of us admired the dishes as we sat down to a traditional Thanksgiving meal in 1999. We made jokes about the much-anticipated, long-postponed, anti-climactic, inaugural meal on the china, and I invoked the heavens and asked Mom if she were finally able to rest in peace. We discussed our preference for modern dishwasher-safe stoneware and Melmac. Why did these women of the past put such importance on owning and maintaining such impractical stuff?

But when that discussion had run its course, we cast cynicism and modern sensibility aside and toasted a by-gone era when dreams of elegance, perfection, and prosperity were possible to a woman who possessed a set of Good Bavarian China.

Child's Play
by Joan Claire Graham

I drove past the park the other day where a gaggle of very small kids, dressed in red and blue uniforms, were playing soccer. Parents, grandparents and siblings lined the sidelines as adults attempted to turn chaos into order, point the tykes in the right direction, and encourage them to kick the ball and not each other. I don't remember ever participating in a play activity supervised by adults when I was a kid.

Like Charlie Brown's friends or the Little Rascals, Minnesota kids of my generation were self sufficient. We had parents, but they didn't enter our play world. They let us play outside without supervision by the time we were three years old. We were allowed to roller skate around the block and walk unchaperoned to school, to the park, to the corner grocery, or to a friend's house. We set up our own Kool-Aid stands and pumped air into the tires of our own bikes. On hot summer days, we'd borrow a couple of picnic blankets, pin them to the clothesline, and make a tent.

When we played a game, we figured out the rules and kept order ourselves. We played ball for the sake of playing, not for the sake of entertaining adults. If someone got hurt, we fixed him. If someone was thirsty, he drank from the hose on the side of the nearest house. If someone's brother was too young to play, we took perverse pleasure in telling him the truth and watching him cry. Not everything about our play was joyful, but we coped and survived.

Any number of boys and girls between the ages of three and twelve joined our neighborhood games all summer as we moved comfortably from one yard to the next. The mothers, all housewives, knew everybody but stayed out of our way. They called us home at suppertime and got angry if we didn't obey promptly. If it wasn't mealtime, mothers let children run unfettered.

Not only kids, but everyone's dogs and cats had the run of the neighborhood. We even befriended the squirrels. Skippy was the librarian's affable brown and tan mutt, and Dickie was a sprightly little gray squirrel. We enjoyed their company and considered them part of the gang. Skippy woke up every afternoon to hang out with the kids while the librarian was at work, and he often sat at someone's feet to get his back scratched with someone's toe.

I don't know who named Dickie, but everyone knew and liked him. He wasn't so bold as to eat out of hands, but he felt comfortable in the company of children. When we'd call his name and make kissing noises, he'd sit up and act interested. When Skippy came around, however, Dickie would make a dash for the nearest elm tree because Skippy chased cars, the city bus, and squirrels. When he'd chase Dickie, we'd chase Skippy. It was our job, after all, to keep order.

Throughout the summer, we witnessed a few close calls, but as the days grew hot, we let down our guard. One day as we hopscotched on the sidewalk, Skippy came tearing out from between the houses, and Dickie took off on his usually successful run up the tree. But this time Skippy ran so fast that he actually ran a ways up the tree. Not expecting this sudden burst of athletic prowess from the dog, Dickie stopped his ascent a bit too soon. Skippy grabbed him by the tail, tore his grip from the bark, and threw him down.

We screamed as Skippy snatched the little squirrel from the ground. Our shrieks scared the dog, and he started to run with Dickie hanging from his mouth, crying for help. We chased Skippy through yards and gardens, but he would not give up his prey. We pelted him with stones, but he would not release Dickie. The poor little squirrel screamed and twisted but was helpless in the jaws of the dog.

After fifteen minutes of high anxiety and heroic determination, we cornered Skippy in a neighbor's garage and pelted him with sticks. We knew better than to get too close to either animal but thought we could intimidate Skippy with noise and numbers. The sticks worked. Skippy dropped Dickie, but the little squirrel was too stunned to know which way to run. In the three seconds it took the panicked animal to somersault this way and that, Skippy snatched him up again, and delivered a mighty shake that broke his neck. Then, his work accomplished, Skippy dropped the limp squirrel and left us to deal with death as he skulked out of the garage and returned to sun himself on the librarian's porch.

No adults noticed or helped as we borrowed a shovel from the garage and dug a hole under the elm. Using the shovel as a pallet, we carried Dickie to his grave, covered him with dirt, and covered the dirt with dandelions. Then, amidst tears and proclamations that we didn't like Skippy any more, we started to plan our retaliation. We would tell the librarian that her dog was a murderer, we would never pet him or scratch his back again, and we would never let him in our yards. Skippy, who had turned our otherwise ordinary innocent day of child's play into a memory, had become the enemy.

I don't think any of us were older than eight. When we told our harrowing story at dinner, our parents clicked their tongues at the pity of it all and praised us for not touching the dead squirrel or getting close enough to allow the dog to bite us.

Today's parents will read this and click their tongues in disbelief that children so young were put in the position of having to deal with such a frightening and dangerous situation. "Where were the parents?" they'll ask. "Couldn't they have intervened? Couldn't they have supervised? Couldn't they have bought the children a new squirrel? Couldn't they have offered something besides words to their poor traumatized children?"

But our parents' words gave us some small comfort, and I honestly don't know what more they could have done. This experience, with its terror and defeat, belonged to the children. We learned a powerful life lesson about victims and predators, and its impact was magnified because we children were allowed to experience the incident and deal with the outcome.

Play resumed after dinner but on a subdued note. For a few days, we took the time to put fresh dandelions on Dickie's grave and to chase Skippy home whenever he came loping across the yard. In time, however, as the hot summer days wore on, we forgot memorials and retaliation as we became immersed again in child's play.

Shop Till You Drop
by Joan Claire Graham

I visited the Mall of America, the shopping Mecca of the world, and came home with the following items: two sore feet, a headache, a refrigerator magnet shaped like the Metrodome, a Lego wrist watch and a Jesse Ventura bumper sticker. The excessiveness of the Mall brought on a case of sensory overload. Did I need anything I bought? Did I see anybody I know? Did my purchases contribute to the welfare of my community? Something was definitely missing from the megamall experience.

As a child, I loved shopping in my hometown, which had a commercial district comparable to that of most towns its size. Downtown Albert Lea was certainly not the international hub of commerce, but it had its charm, and shoppers bought everything they needed from merchants who knew their names. Many townsfolk could walk downtown and back in less time than it takes to park a car and find it again at the Mall of America, and downtown was a social gathering place and hub of community activity. I think most small town residents enjoyed and appreciated their downtowns, and when local merchants were nudged out by discount chains, the pennies saved on purchases failed to compensate for the loss of an important part of our lives.

Stores stayed open Friday night until 9 and closed on Sunday. Window dressers clothed mannequins in the latest merchandise, coordinated by color, design, or theme. Career clerks sometimes informed customers by phone that merchandise they might like had just arrived or had been marked down. Although local shops were architecturally diverse and offered personalized service, they were replaced by discount stores that all look alike and megamalls staffed by part-time clerks who act like they can't wait until it's time to go home.

Most small cities had at least one local department store,

Woolworth's, and Montgomery Wards. An assortment of other local, regional, and national stores lined a couple of blocks of every town's main street, but now most have closed. I recognized few downtown businesses when I returned to Albert Lea a few years ago, but memories of the old days are vivid.

Skinner Chamberlain, Southern Minnesota's Largest and Finest Department Store, boasted five floors of merchandise ranging from groceries to furniture. To a child, Skinners was a wonderland. For starters, the store had a drinking fountain. On a hot day, a kid could walk past a row of molded plastic legs wearing nylon stockings and clear jars filled with lavender and jasmine scented powder, turn left after the elevator and enjoy a cold drink. Between the elevator and the drinking fountain was a stairway with a lookout window at the second landing where a child could view the entire first floor of Skinners from a few feet up.

Clerks did not have to count change. Instead, they wrote up the transaction on a little note pad and stuffed the note and the customer's money into a little silver car that was part of a wonderful aerial railroad system that crisscrossed the store's upper atmosphere. The clerk would attach the silver car to the system and give it a little boost, propelling it along cables, around corners, dodging other little cars from other departments, and finally disappearing into an office where someone we couldn't see would stuff change into the little car and send it back along the track to the right clerk. Since we had very few other amusements in Albert Lea, we kids loved to watch that little silver cable car.

In the mid-fifties, Skinners installed in their shoe department a mechanical wooden horse with a real leather saddle. I became an equestrian, and after spending my appropriated dime, I'd sit on the horse and look so pathetic that strangers would take pity on me and put more dimes into the slot.

The horse was not the only mechanical phenomenon at Skinners. Every kid in town loved to ride the escalator that carried customers all the way to the second floor and dumped them off in front of the beauty salon. Customers going to the furniture department on the fourth floor or the Green Stamps redemption center on the third floor had to cut through ladies' apparel and take the elevator or the stairs the rest of the way up. The elevator was staffed by an operator whom kids all thought had the most fascinating job in town.

Another recreational opportunity at Skinners was located in the dry goods department. While mothers sat on wooden swivel stools to study the latest pattern books from McCalls and Simplicity, kids spun around on adjacent stools until the store appeared to be revolving. Some kids sat, while others spun on their stomachs.

I first met Santa Claus in Skinners' basement, and I have a picture to prove it. As he boosted me up on his lap, I looked at the blue pinstripe shirt showing beneath his Santa suit and said, "My dad has a shirt just like that. I don't think you are Santa." The picture captures my skepticism.

My mother committed a crime at Skinners but never served time. She was pricing cat food in their grocery department when she looked out the window and saw her bus approaching. She sprinted out the door in a panic and made it across the street just in time, but when she breathlessly reached for her bus money, she realized she was still holding the can of cat food. When she returned to Skinners the next day to pay the fourteen cents, the clerk said he'd noticed her transgression but, knowing my mother, thought it was an honest mistake. How embarrassing it would have been to have had Big Ole, the sheriff, stop the bus and haul my mom off to the slammer for stealing a can of Puss 'n Boots!

Skinners was Albert Lea's largest and finest department store, but Montgomery Wards was pretty big too. Their original store on Broadway sold everything from shovels to socks. Shoppers who stopped to pick up catalog orders stayed to browse through the retail departments. I have four great memories of Wards.

First: Monkey Wards, as everybody always called it, had an ice skate exchange in their basement where kids could sell last year's skates and buy a new used pair for a nominal handling fee. Wooden bins helped sort skates by size and type. What a deal!

Second: When I was five, I won a three-dollar gift certificate from Wards in the Parks Department doll buggy parade. I thought the prize was a bust until my mom took me to the shoe department where I selected a pair of striped elastic sandals which I wore all summer. There was credit left to buy a couple of new pairs of underpants. The clerk made a big fuss over me and praised me for winning the prize. I didn't tell her that my mom did all the work decorating the doll buggy.

Third: My mother liked to tell the story about when she moved to Albert Lea during World War II. Since cotton was rationed, a welcomer from the store phoned the new town resident and asked if she'd like to be on Ward's sheet list. "Your what?" Mom asked incredulously.

Fourth: We had a legendary family incident at Wards. Mother took my brother Michael shopping when he was a toddler and made the mistake of turning her back. He crawled out of his Taylor Tot when he spotted a woman wearing a fur coat. The woman was intent on examining merchandise on a table so didn't notice his little hands petting her coat.

Enjoying the fur texture and getting a bit bolder, Michael picked up the bottom of the coat and popped it over his head. At this point the woman felt violated, stood up, and started to swish from side to side looking for the person under her coat. Michael became frightened in that churning dark chamber and did the only thing he felt he could do. He grabbed the woman's leg with his chubby hands and bit her in the butt. The woman screamed and lunged, my brother fell to the floor crying, customers formed a circle, and the manager came to quell the commotion. My mother always said it was her most embarrassing moment of motherhood.

Completing the lineup of Albert Lea's three major stores was Woolworth's. Whether a shopper wanted to browse, buy merchandise, or enjoy lunch, Woolworths' was the place to go. Their lunch counter served everything from banana splits and apple dumplings to full course dinners. Menu items and prices were pictured high on the wall facing customers. Diners on stools at the counter were supposed to obey the "No Tipping" sign. I was a teenager before I realized "No Tipping" didn't mean you should refrain from spilling your lemonade. Drinks like lemonade and orange punch always looked delicious drooling down the inside of a rectangular aerator that pumped colorful liquid up from the center and down the insides.

Woolworth's sold a fascinating array of merchandise that included parakeets, fish, turtles, records, dish pans, playing cards, kites, balls, dolls, puzzles, falsies, makeup, jewelry, ash trays, knitting supplies, yard goods, powder puffs, shoulder pads, string, school supplies, scrap books, oil cloth, extension cords, May baskets, Easter baskets, Valentines, Christmas cards and Bobbsey Twin Books. Occasionally a demonstrator with a flair for theatrics would entertain shoppers with a pitch for a new chopper, a revolutionary mending device, or a glue to mend broken dishes, and during Holy Week, Woolworths hired someone to write names with icing on hollow chocolate eggs.

Candies--chocolate stars, orange smiles, M & M's, circus peanuts, corn candy, malted milk balls, chocolate covered raisins and peanuts, jelly beans and gum drops-- were displayed temptingly in cases, weighed to the customer's order, and scooped into a white bag. Selecting candy required five or six laps around the cases. I envied candy counter clerks as much as elevator operators.

The three big stores formed the core of the downtown area while smaller department and specialty stores offered most Albert Leans everything they could ever want. Ben Franklin sold toys and candy, Wee Walker baby shoes, crafts, turtles with floral decals on their shells, parakeets, and a few clothing items.

I bought my first bra at Ben Franklin's, a 32AA that cost 79 cents. Mom hadn't noticed my blossoming womanhood, but she took the news of my purchase so well that she let me go back the next day and buy a second bra, proving the old adage that you can never own too many high quality bras.

On the west side of the street, Spurgeons sold an odd assortment of cheap clothes, luggage, electric organs, and candy. Three Sisters sold can-can slips called fifty yard sweeps, and locally owned jewelry stores like Braaten's added a touch of class with their tastefully simple window displays.

Wallace's, which had another money trolley, sold nice clothes for ladies and children as well as yard goods, sheets, and accessories for the home. Merchandise went home in red Wallace plaid bags or complimentary gift wrapping. Upstairs, in a balcony at the back, the store displayed ladies' hats and gloves. All the cool high school girls bought pleated skirts and sweaters designed by Bobbie Brooks at Wallace's or across the street at Stevenson's.

Everybody bought Buster Browns and Kickerinos at Bisgaard's or Plymouth Shoes, but kids started summer with a pair of blue or red tennies purchased for three dollars at J.C. Penney. Teens bought jeans, dads bought work clothes, and moms patronized Penney's January White Sale. Sanders' Drug sold books in their basement. Merrill sold popcorn from a trailer, and Kieffer's Cigar Store sold root beer in frosted glasses. Gordon's sold appliances, Countryman sold movie magazines, and Leuthold's or Gildner Lagesson fitted a suit to every boy transitioning into manhood,

On side streets, Coast to Coast, Gambles, Westrum Outlet, Busy Bee Shoe repair, Stephenson's Music, Russell's Toys and Gretchen's Sweets completed the full line of goods and services available in Albert Lea.

Christmas shopping was heralded in late November with evergreen swags, lights, and red bells strung across Broadway. Nobody knew the cheerless women who leaned from green Salvation Army huts from Thanksgiving till Christmas, wearing storm coats and bomber hats and incessantly ringing bells I can still hear, but we accepted their presence as a temporary part of our lives. In spring, merchants installed several blocks of wooden track on which shoppers lined up donated dimes to help the March of Dimes find a cure for polio.

At the end of summer, clerks hauled clearance merchandise out to the sidewalk, dressed in crazy outfits, and celebrated Ridiculous Days. We felt we had a personal stake in local commerce because we knew the folks with whom we were doing business. They attended our churches, cheered the local teams, sponsored charity drives, sold grandstand tickets, and sent their children to our schools.

Times changed, and old merchants locked their doors and yielded to Walmart and others who built slick stores on the outskirts of town. Bar codes and scanners replaced money trolleys, and the career clerk who took pride in helping customers she knew by name became a relic of the past. Kids who used to be amused by a one-story escalator, a mechanical horse, and swivel stools grew up and took their kids to ride the roller coaster at Camp Snoopy. Huge conglomerate commerce centers replaced all but a few small community businesses.

The Mall of America has a thousand times more goods than anybody could ever need, but can shoppers find what they want? Can they do business with folks they know or care about? Can they contribute to the prosperity of the community where their children play and attend school? Folks can shop till they drop, but they may come home feeling like I did--dazed and unsatisfied--because the megamall isn't really about community, commerce or need. It's about big time glitter, excess, and greed.

Imaginary Friends
by Joan Claire Graham

I think of my early childhood as a time spent in solitude. Maybe all children, intent on the formidable task of discovering the universe, think of themselves as solo acts and focus on their inner world. I know I did. My brother was four years older than I, and although we shared a few common interests like Roy Rogers and Hopalong Cassidy, he and I did not get along. Since sharing time with him resulted in physical conflict followed by corporal punishment, I pretty much tried to stay out of his way. Since he thought I was a dork, he pretty much went along with that plan.

As a way of coping with life on my own, I created five imaginary friends named Mister, Seedy, Patrickson, Peekhole, and Morgan Spelvin. I can't write those names today without smiling because the five together look to me like members of a law firm that specializes in handling criminal cases caused by other members of the firm.

We didn't commit crimes, but we had adventures in my mind. Like Saturday cliffhangers at the Rivoli Theatre, our adventures were serialized. They ended when I ran out of ideas and started again when I thought of a new twist. I'd usually sign off by saying something like, "Tune in tomorrow if you want to know what happens next."

I don't know who I thought would be tuning in because I never shared my scenarios with anybody besides the six of us. When my mother heard me talking to myself, I'd shake off her queries with disclaimers. No, that must have been someone else she heard talking in my room. Maybe it was the radio.

Although they were all male, Mister, Seedy, Patrickson, Peekhole and Morgan Spelvin had distinct personalities, and none actually lived in our house. They came to see me from places as near as the rosebush between our house and the Johnsons' and from as far as the house with the green door next to the place by the lake where my mother's chiropractor lived. Sometimes they all came at once, and sometimes only one could make it. When one was absent, we often talked about him and wished he could be there. Sometimes he showed up and surprised the rest of us.

Although it's probably not fair to pick favorites, I think mine was Mister. Since he lived so near, he was able to play often. I don't know how he managed to tolerate all those thorns in the bush where he lived or how he stayed alive during Minnesota winters, but he, like all the others, always went home after playing. Sometimes I stood at the window and watched him leave, and sometimes I talked to him through the frosty pane. Sometimes I got caught chatting with Mister. When I got older and my mother recalled my behavior, I denied any recollection.

One adventure involved a scheme to take scrap lumber my dad had in the basement and make napkin holders. I don't know whose idea this was, but it turned out to be a bad one. After finding the wood and opening the paint, we all realized that none of us knew how to operate a hammer or saw. Not only that, but we had absolutely no idea how to turn a board into a napkin holder. I ended up spilling paint on my clothes, and Mister, Seedy, Patrickson, Peekhole and Morgan Spelvin ran home. I was the only one who got caught, and I cried as my dad's big hand paddled my little butt. How could I explain to him what I had been trying to do? We had wanted to surprise him with our shiny new napkin holders.

Not all our adventures were calamitous. The guys and I enjoyed listening to records. My mother won a 78 rpm portable record player in a drawing at Stephenson's Music Store so I knew how to use the machine, and I owned dozens of little records. Some of these were plastic coated colorful cardboard disks, and others were yellow plastic records made by the same company that published Little Golden Books. We'd sit by the record player for hours sorting the records and discussing which one to play next. Once we'd made our decision, we'd open up full throttle to sing along with the great recordings of songs like "Laugh, Laugh, Phonograph," "Green for Go, Red for Stop," "Don't Put Things in Your Mouth," and "Billy's House Has All Burned Down." When my mother asked why I had to sing so loudly, I would laugh and tell my friends to pipe down.

Fantasy sometimes commingled with reality. A prowler broke into our house the night Cedric Adams performed onstage at the high school auditorium. All adults in the neighborhood attended the show while the prowler helped himself to the contents of their jewelry boxes. Of course, nobody in Albert Lea locked their doors in those days. A woman who rented our fourth bedroom was supposed to be babysitting, but she was in her room with the door shut as I heard heavy steps coming up the stairs.

As luck would have it, Mister had stopped in to keep me company in my solitary room that night. As we heard the footsteps, I asked, "Hey, Mister, who do you think that is coming up the stairs?"

Mister replied in a different voice. "Your dad should be home by now. Let's go ask him if he knows. " At this point, the sound of the footsteps stopped and then receded as the would-be burglar turned around and fled the scene. The next morning, Big Ole and the other cops surmised that I had frightened the thief away since he had absconded with a big haul from the homes of several neighbors.

When I started kindergarten in 1951, I was disappointed to discover that none of the guys were in my class. As the weeks went by, their visits became less frequent, and then one day they stopped. Like Puff the Magic Dragon, they had frolicked in the autumn mist in a land called Albert Lea. But when they were replaced by real playmates, Mister, Seedy, Patrickson, Peekhole and Morgan Spelvin sailed away and yielded to friends whom everyone could see.

Curtain Up, Light the Lights!
by Joan Claire Graham

Albert Lea High School Auditorium was a magical place when I was growing up in the fifties and sixties. In its heyday, it seated nearly two thousand spectators in comfortable padded seats on the main floor and in the balcony. An old statue of Colonel Albert Lea guarded the lobby, and the ticket booth housed an elaborate system of tiny cubbies that held tickets for reserved seat productions. Kids believed the best seats were in the first rows of the balcony where they could see and be seen, but management closed the balcony unless crowd size warranted opening it. Albert Lea Auditorium saw many capacity crowds.

The stage, which was about fifty feet wide and thirty feet deep, accommodated plays, bands, graduation ceremonies, orchestras, ballets, and choral groups. The velvet proscenium curtain opened slowly, and spotlights, focused steeply from a crow's nest in the auditorium ceiling, followed onstage action. The unfinished upstage surface gave dancers traction, and a tattered professionally painted backdrop hung across the back wall. The sound system was nearly nonexistent when I was a kid, and air conditioning was unheard of, but I fell in love with live entertainment in that auditorium. Sitting there, as the houselights dimmed, was like experiencing *West Side Story's* lyrics, "Something's coming, something big." Anticipation made hearts beat faster.

Many towns had large auditoriums that functioned as entertainment venues and social gathering places, but Albert Lea's was especially nice. When spectators went to an event at the auditorium, they dressed up. During intermission, when they talked to friends and neighbors, they practiced civility and good manners. Auditorium events were special occasions.

The Civic Music Association booked a variety of entertainment that included the National Ballet of Canada, the Minnesota Orchestra and the Vienna Boys' Choir. Ferrante and Teischer performed there before and after "Theme From the Apartment" became a big hit, Fred Waring and his Pennsylvanians sang familiar tunes, and Isaac Stern and David Rubinoff played violins on that stage. Marian Anderson's rich contralto voice filled the hall one night, and Beverly Sills brought to Albert Lea a taste of the Metropolitan Opera. George Shearing and Charlie Byrd played jazz, and local folks proudly welcomed home Charles Schneider and Katherine Jacobson when they came back as a concert pianists.

Musical and dramatic acts advertised with placards in store windows, radio announcements and newspaper ads, and crowds of Albert Leans showed up. The St. Olaf Choir, the St. Mary's Marinotes, and the Augsburg Players performed there, as did the South Dakota Passion Play.

In December, high school choir director Bob Myers wowed crowds with his candlelight Christmas Concert. Robed choir members carrying battery powered candles marched in to "Oh Come All Ye Faithful." After the traditional carols, with hundreds of kids onstage or lining the aisles, Myers played eight piano chords, and on each chord, one eighth of the candles flickered out.

When band director Cap Emmons retired in the early sixties, townsfolk filled the auditorium one Sunday afternoon and paid tribute. The emcee showed a film on the big screen, and an alumni band dusted off their old trombones and had another go at "El Capitan." Emmons had conducted concerts there for thirty years, but never to a more appreciative crowd.

High school students produced two or three plays each year and conducted pep rallies with skits and cheers. The school sponsored educational assemblies with motivational speakers, travelogues, or science presentations.

At the Homecoming assembly, the student body sat tense before closed curtains, awaiting the unveiling of the queen. As the piano began the opening strains of "La Czarine," the chorus sang,

"Praise and homage to our noble queen, lovely queen............. '

Then the curtain swept open, and chorus members stifled their screams of surprise so they could sing the name of the queen who sat clutching roses and wearing a tiara. If her name was something like Barbara Jean, it fit right into the song, "La Czarine," but a name like Marilyn Elizabeth or Gretchen Abigail had to be crammed into that song with a wedge and hammer.

The annual Tigers Roar talent show played several evenings each January to packed houses. Tap dancers, accordionists, classical pianists, barbershop quartets, novelty dances and the swing band were staple acts, but some forward looking individuals and groups broke tradition with renditions of current hits by popular artists. I heard my first live Rock and Roll in the late fifties at the Tigers Roar when Steve Leuthold played to an enthusiastic crowd.

Graduation ceremonies moved to Southwest Gymnasium in the sixties when classes grew too large, but high school baccalaureate ceremonies continued in the auditorium until they fell from grace. The last time I stood on that stage was at my senior awards ceremony, and the last time I sat in the auditorium was in 1974 when I attended my sister's high school production of *You're a Good Man, Charlie Brown.*

I typed "Albert Lea High School Auditorium" into a search engine yesterday to find information for this memory, and I'm still in a state of shock. I downloaded a beautiful picture of the entire house taken from the stage. I was glad to see the old place has held up so well, but my shock came from the context of the web site. The auditorium is for sale! Albert Lea High School, once the hub of the city, has closed. A new school now sits on the other side of town, and the old school and auditorium are being sold to the highest bidder. Realtors suggest that the property might be reconfigured for condos or assisted living facilities, and I'm still dismayed.

I hope whoever buys the property has respect for history and preserves that wonderful old auditorium whose walls have echoed so much music, laughter, and applause over the years. It would be a shame to tear it down or turn it into something stupid like an indoor flea market or a climbing wall for would-be rock climbers.

The auditorium's fate shouldn't affect me because I don't live in Albert Lea any more. However, I have been thinking of it a lot lately. It was an important part of the community where I grew up because the events it housed gave us culture, excitement, and a glimpse of something beyond our everyday lives. I hadn't intended to go home again, but I wanted that auditorium to be there in case I ever changed my mind.

The Little Box Camera
by Joan Claire Graham

Mother brought along her little box camera to family events that could be photographed outdoors. The camera, which was a little bigger than a pound of butter, had a dimpled black leatherette case and a strap handle. It was compact and simple with no adjustments, no color film, and one shutter speed. Since there was no flash attachment, the family marked special occasions by traipsing outside to pose squinting into the sun. If the weather was cold, we wore coats. Since each roll of film held only eight shots, those who were photographed had only one chance to look their best. After lining up her subjects, Mother held the camera in front of her, looked down into the view finder, and clicked the shutter with a button on the right. Despite these severe limitations, my mother took some great pictures with that little box camera.

Although she proved her photographic talent quite well at birthday parties, confirmations, and baptisms, Mom did her best work at the lake, which was in Ely. The lake pictures, unlike the others, were candid and casual. Mother followed her subjects around and caught them doing interesting things.

My parents, grandmother, brother and I vacationed at the lake every summer until I was six. Mom spent the first day cleaning the cabin because no matter how clean the cabin was when we got there, it never met her high standards. After a day of scrubbing and scouring, Mother would grab her little box camera and take us kids out to splash around the dock, catch minnows in a hair net, or ride in the boat. By her calculations, we had about two days to enjoy the place before my dad got sick of fishing and started agitating to go home. Despite the fact that we rented cabins by the week, Dad's anxiety always forced us home after four or five days.

The photos Mother took at Lake Ely trigger quintessential Minnesota memories. She allowed herself only one roll of film per vacation, but she took some terrific pictures. One shows little me, dressed down to my ankles in a life jacket, holding a northern pike half my size. My brother and I float in inner tubes in another, and in the next, my blonde curls shine in the sun as I watch my dad clean a fish. With my arm around my brother, I am caught forever in the only moment of peaceful coexistence the two of us ever enjoyed. What great photographs!

I have always treasured those pictures Mom took at the lake, and I am grateful that she preserved a few moments of my Minnesota childhood on film. One afternoon, however, she took the picture that plagued me throughout the rest of my childhood. I distinctly remember that day at the lake, although I was less than two years old.

Because it was cumbersome, I wriggled out of my cold, wet, woolen swimsuit. With my little tin Easter bucket, I decided to take all the water from one side of the dock and dump it into the lake on the other side. Although the transfer of Lake Ely from one side of the dock to the other was a formidable task, I was determined to do it.

I filled my little bucket and doggedly climbed over the dock to empty it several times. During one such trip, Mom waded into the water, stood behind me, and snapped the perfect photo. Although my body blocks the little bucket, my face and body language show determination, focus, and a sense of purpose as the sun beats down on my back and creates shiny patterns on the shallow water.

Mom's friends thought the picture was good enough to earn a prize in a contest, so Mom ordered copies and enlargements. She never got around to sending it in to a contest, but she never got tired of showing that picture to people and basking in their praise. "Go get that picture of you at the lake," she'd tell me, and I'd obediently but reluctantly oblige.

As I grew out of the baby stage, I found that picture to be a source of embarrassment. When I'd protest showing off my bare butt to photo critics, Mom would say, "Don't be silly. You were only a baby!" Since I could distinctly remember the photo shoot, I couldn't see any difference between the baby in the picture and the ten year old protesting Mom's showing the photo to admiring friends and relatives. When people looked at that picture of my bare cheeks, I felt my other cheeks heat up with a blush.

I tried hiding the picture a few times, but Mom had several copies as well as the negative. Those pictures were like the *500 Hats of Bartholomew Cubbins*. When one disappeared, another popped up. Eventually, however, Mom either stopped showing the picture to folks or else she had the sense to show it when I wasn't around.

Mom lost interest in photography when I was eight or nine years old. My brother and I took over as family photographers when we became old enough to shoot pictures with Brownie Star Flash cameras of our own. We used Sylvania Blue Dot flashbulbs and shot dozens of rolls of color film, but none of our pictures turned out very well. Our subjects either had red eyes or they looked like they were caught in the headlights. My mom used to critique our work, furrow her brow, and observe, "You know, that little box camera we used to have took the best pictures." She was right; it took good pictures, but I think the bulk of the credit should go to the photographer.

I never knew my grandfather, but I have always lived with a beautiful wedding portrait taken August 13, 1907. Elmer and Clara Eaton, seated, and their wedding party. p. 27

Dear Snookums and Muggins, p. 29
Aquinata and Albert Eaton, age 6 & 8

In 1905 my grandmother and three female cousins set out from their prosperous southern Minnesota homes in order to stake homestead claims in the wilds of North Dakota. p. 27

Lex (left) possessed impulsiveness in contrast to Mom's obsessively practical restraint. Lex was a doer while Mom was a dreamer. p. 13

The Ford company posted a quote in their showroom, My mother, reflected in the Ford dealership window, copies the quote as I pose with a friend p. 43

Skippy woke up every afternoon to hang out with the kids while the librarian was at work. p. 59

Susannah looked like a little princess sitting in her pretty wagon. (Note: missing rear hubcap.) p. 6

"Wait a minute! Those are my sand box toys!" The last time I'd played with them had been years ago. p. 91

He crawled out of his Taylor Tot when he spotted a woman wearing a fur coat. p. 65

You see, in addition to living in a small Minnesota town, my family was Catholic, and the only thing more oppressive than being a Catholic back then in that town was going to the Catholic school. First Communion Class, 1954 p. 15

The Grahams, consisting of two Irish grandparents, seven children, and eighteen grandchildren, got together every summer at Uncle Bob's farm in Henderson. The farm kids were a fun-loving and rowdy bunch who found joy in teaching their city cousins how to do things we had never imagined possible--like rock an outhouse while someone was inside or hypnotize a chicken. p. 34

Mom's friends thought this picture was good enough to earn a prize in a contest, so Mom ordered copies and enlargements. She never got around to sending it in to a contest, but she never got tired of showing that picture to people and basking in their praise. "Go get that picture of you at the lake," she'd tell me, and I'd obediently but reluctantly oblige. p. 77

Previously, most travelers had enjoyed cabin courts and hotels, but the idea of parking your car by your room, conveniently unloading your luggage, and being attended to by a person in a front office gave rise to a new term: motoring +hotel gave us "motel." Dad and Mother were quite successful because they worked 24 hours a day, 7 days a week, 52 weeks a year. p. 116

I learned to love the smell of gasoline and truly admired my dad's starched uniform with its Texaco Oil insignia p. 115

Dad always said, "You know, your mother was a real beauty," and that much we knew, but he never told me more. p. 121

Anticipating Christmas because it meant heading to Daytons in Minneapolis to stand in line for hours to see Santa.   p. 135

While Dad was stationed at Truex Field in Madison, Wisconsin, I was born. p. 121

Hope School District 12, Mrs. Fleener's 5th through 8th grade, 1953-54.   p. 92
Row 1: Dorothy Schiller, Judy Schuster, Margaret Steele, Shirley Noske, Carol Pike, Laura Burshem, Peggy Metcalf, Ginny Wesley. Row 2: Duane Wobschall, Jesse Pike, Eddie Srsen, Chuck Srsen, Billy Metcalf, Donny Johnson, Sallie Ribbe

My first car decorated for homecoming. It was a '36 Hupmobile we pasted with cut-out dots so we could dress up as clowns and throw candy at the spectators
p. 113

Co-author Joan Claire Graham's prom ensemble from 1964

Dressing for the senior prom, co-author Kathy Megyeri wore a strapless dress with at least 5 crinolines beneath it.

The most memorable event of my first ten years was the Owatonna Centennial celebration which occurred during May and June, 1954. The normally tranquil town was suddenly teeming with men in beards and women in sunbonnets. p. 97

Pontoppidan was more than a church. It was one of the two social centers of the community (the other being the schoolhouse) p. 100

Red Light People
by Jennifer Laura Paige

My kindergarten class sat Indian style on the story rug in front of a square movie screen that rolled up and down like a window shade. Mrs. Ferris opened a flat, circular container and loaded its contents onto projector #3, which someone had rolled into the classroom on a square cart and parked behind us. As she threaded the projector, she announced that we'd be watching a movie today.

Students waved their hands in the air, bracing their raised hands with their opposite arms for support and emphasis. After a few seconds, their patience wore thin, and they shouted out their questions anyway.

"Can it be *Star Wars*?"

"Is it going to be the *Muppet Movie*?"

"Did you know that my house has a walk-in basement?"

"I want to watch *Star Wars*! Please, Please, Please?"

Mrs. Ferris laughed and shook her head. "No, no, settle down. It's not going to be a movie you've seen before. This is a very special movie."

"Is it S*tar Wars*?"

"No. It's a very important movie that's only shown in schools. It's about safety. Now, does anyone know what a stranger is?"

Answers erupted amid Mrs. Ferris' protests of "Raised hands, please."

"Jeremy!"

"Darth Vadar!"

"Kidnappers!"

"There's a walk-in basement where I live!"

"Kenny, wait for Show-and-Tell. We can hear about your basement then." Mrs. Ferris said, "Now I heard a lot of interesting answers, but I don't think I heard the right answer. A stranger is a person, in real life, whom you don't know. Jeremy is not a stranger to us because he is in our class. We know him. Darth Vadar is a character in a movie, but he's not the type of stranger we're likely to run into every day here in Robbinsdale.

"Now, a few of you said 'kidnappers,' and that's closer to the right answer, but not quite. You see, most strangers are nice people, just like you, me, your mom, and your dad. But there are some bad strangers who like to harm little children, and that is why we're going to watch this movie about why it is bad to talk to strangers."

I was shocked. The concept that it was bad to talk to strangers was completely new to me. I talked to strangers all the time. I'd approach them on the bus and in supermarket checkout lines. I'd tell them about my day, what I'd had for breakfast, or what color underwear I was wearing. I'd tell them about the musical I'd written and offer to sing an excerpt. After reading a picture book about human reproduction called *Where Did I Come From?*, I'd been unable to pass a pregnant woman on the street without proudly informing her that I knew how she'd gotten that way.

Mrs. Ferris dimmed the lights and started the projector. I was one of the few kindergartners who could read the title: *The Red Light People.* The film opens with a child walking home from school on a sunny day. A benign-looking woman pulls up in a station wagon. "Hey, there, Susie! Your mom's been in an accident, and I'm a good friend of hers. She asked me to come pick you up and take you to the hospital." The child hesitates as the camera freezes on the woman's face, which is taking on a newly malevolent appearance. Percussive violin music blares as the stranger's face is quickly intercut with images of a flashing red traffic light and the words, "RED LIGHT, RED LIGHT, RED LIGHT." My heart pounded in abject terror as I watched this unsuspecting child about to fall prey to one of the Red Light People.

According to the film, Red Light People were everywhere. They looked just like regular people and often appeared friendly. Red Light People approached small children in parks and on sidewalks asking for directions or help finding a lost puppy. Disguised as a family friend or traveling salesmen, they knocked on doors of latchkey children or offered toys or candy to unsuspecting children. Then the startling music and flashes of red indicated this was not a nice grown-up, but a Red Light Person. As scenes of child entrapment by Red Light People unfolded, I grew more and more horrified.

We never saw what the Red Light People actually did once they caught children in their traps, but I didn't need details. Instinctively I knew that the ominous designs of Red Light People must exceed any evil I had ever seen or imagined. Their frozen faces bathed in flashing red light filled me with the bone chilling terror--the terror of the unknown.

Although the movie offered suggestions like family passwords to ensure safety, I knew these flimsy weapons would be ineffective in the war with evil of the type that I had just witnessed.

After watching the film, I anticipated the end of the school day with dread. At noon, when kindergarten ended, I would have to leave the relatively safe confines of my classroom and walk home through 4 blocks that I now knew to be infested with terrifyingly undetectable Red Light People.

When the time came, I ran three blocks without stopping, until I ran out of breath. As I stood red-faced and panting on the sidewalk a block from home, a burly man in an old pick-up truck pulled to a stop. Even though he didn't look like the Red Light People in the movie, I knew instinctively that he was one of them. He paused for a second before throwing a beer can and a cigarette butt out his truck window. That was all the proof I needed.

"Red Light! Red Light!" I screamed. My coattails trailed behind me as I raced, frantic to escape from this man. My sides ached and I gasped for breath, but I didn't stop and I didn't look back. This was the first of many times I would see crimson light flash across the face of a stranger and run with desperation toward the safety of my front door. My fear had been awakened; now I lived in a world inhabited by Red Light People.

A Child's Recollection of Moving Day
by Jennifer Laura Paige

The day we moved was sunny, unusually warm March Minnesota weather. The moving truck driver, a wiry, chain-smoking man in his late twenties, spent the whole day cursing and muttering under his breath, lamenting the unexpected heat wave. The other movers were friends of the family who were just helping out, and they didn't seem to mind. At least, they didn't complain. Some of them worked on loading the seven tons of boxes into the van while others cleaned our house after the furniture was gone.

Being only ten, I didn't have to do much of anything except keep out of the way. I sat on the front stoop, a vantage point from which I could watch the movers but avoid being stepped on or tripped over. The movers meant nothing to me. My father's new job in California didn't concern me either. Even now, hours before we left, moving was still nothing more than a vague possibility. I couldn't imagine it happening, and I was confident that someone would rush in at the last minute shouting, "No! Wait! You can't move to California because.........." I knew they'd have a good reason to keep us in the only place I'd ever lived.

My thoughts were interrupted by the impatient shout of the truck driver. "Hey, Lady, I don't got room for all your junk in my truck. You gotta get rid of some of it or we ain't going anywhere."

My mother inspected the truck. It was indeed packed. She looked from piles of boxes still on the curb to the bored looking driver. "If you had kept your part of the agreement and given us two thirds of the truck instead of only half, this never would have happened," she snapped.

The driver yawned. "Don' look at me. I just drive this here thing. You got a problem, you can talk to my supervisor." He blew a thin ring of smoke into my mother's face. She turned wearily to the group of movers.

"Would anybody like a lawn mower?" Someone nodded in favor of the lawn mower.

"How about a weed-whacker? Maybe we can leave these sandbox toys for the new owners."

I ran up to them in protest. "Wait a minute! Those are my sand box toys!" The last time I'd played with them had been years ago.

My mother whispered for my grandfather to take me inside for a while until things were straightened out with the movers. I was struck by the dramatic change that had come over the house. Our usually cluttered home was empty and spotless. It was then that I realized that moving was real, definite.

As I walked into my empty bedroom, I began to sob uncontrollably. My grandfather tried to comfort me, but I didn't want comforting; I wanted to cry and be miserable.

By the time our car pulled away from our house, it was no longer sunny, but between light and dark--sort of gray. I cried until sleep rescued me as we drove away from that house forever.

The youngest contributor, Jennifer Laura Paige lives in Minneapolis, where she is an actress, writer, and University of Minnesota medical transcriptionist.

Country School 1949-1957
By Margaret Steele Johnson

I was six and a half years old when I started school. Since there was no kindergarten in country school, I went right into first grade at Hope School. District 12 was a little different from other country schools. First, it was in the town of Hope as opposed to being out in the country. Second, it had two classrooms instead of just one. The little room contained grades 1 through 4, and the big room housed grades 5 through 8. Each room had one teacher and from fifteen to twenty students.

I should explain that Hope was not really a town but a group of houses and businesses along one street that was about six blocks long. When my family moved from the farm into "town," it was said the population leaped from 92 to 96.

There were six or seven of us in first grade, and Miss Crane was our teacher. Mrs. Tucker taught second, third, and fourth grades. In fourth grade, Laura Burshem and Shirley Noske joined Carol Pike and me, and we four girls comprised the whole class through eighth grade. Carol and I went through twelve years of school together so it seems ironic that she owns a flower shop in the same town where I now live.

Three cement steps led up to the main entrance of the square white board building. Inside the double doors were a half dozen steps with a railing in the middle separating the entrance to the two classrooms. Off the back of each classroom was a cloakroom where we hung our outerwear on hooks. Girls wore dresses so when it was cold, we wore slacks underneath our skirts for warmth. What a hassle it was to take off and put on those slacks without letting the boys see our underpants!

Off the front of each classroom was a library. Being an avid reader, I quickly read all the books in the little room and couldn't wait to get to the big room to read the rest of the books.

Every fall, I looked forward to the new books we would get, and by fifth grade, a county bookmobile stopped at our school regularly to keep me supplied. I don't recall going to the Owatonna Library much, probably because we didn't go into town often enough to return whatever books we borrowed.

Off the back hall were two bathrooms, each with two flush toilets in stalls and one sink. When I started school, we still had outdoor facilities at home so flush toilets were something I remember about school.

Downstairs, in a cement basement, we had recess when the weather was bad. I remember games like "Captain, May I?", pum-pum-pullaway, and dodge ball. The furnace went out often, so we had to sit at our desks with coats on, but classes went on as usual. Our parents brought us to school every day with lunch packed in lunchboxes and thermos bottles decorated with pictures of Roy Rogers or Dale Evans. Later, we got electric burners to heat up soup, and at some point, milk was delivered. The Mothers' Club (our version of PTA) took turns providing hot lunches about once a month.

Each room had windows along one wall and blackboards on the other. Four rows of desks were screwed to two long strips of wood attached to the floor. Classes met around a table and chairs at the front.

A U.S. flag hung on one side of the front blackboard with a number of rolled maps mounted above it. A large globe stood to one side near the teacher's desk.

A typical daily schedule began with the Pledge of Allegiance. Then classes began with the youngest group first. They got their assignment and went back to their desks to work while the next class went up to the table. Subjects included reading, math, social studies, geography, history (sixth grade always included Minnesota history), spelling, grammar, and literature. My favorite time of day occurred when the teacher read a book chapter to the whole room. I heard or read all the Laura Ingalls Wilder books.

Most of my memories are of the big room where Mrs. Fleener taught fifth grade, and Mrs. Christensen taught all the rest of my country school grades. By eighth grade, I had already listened to the other classes, so it was almost a repeat. It must have been hard for teachers to come up with new activities for fifteen kids in four grades all in the same room.

Extracurricular activities consisted of parties and events at school. With homes so far apart, few kids went trick or treating, which meant that Halloween parties were a big deal. Our mothers made our costumes and provided us with homemade treats. Halloween was a time for pranksters who liked to attack the school. Sometimes they moved the outhouse to the front steps, but one year we found a manure spreader in front of the door!

We spent December practicing for the Christmas program held at Hope Hall on the second floor over the Hope Creamery and Meat Lockers. It was one big room with a wood floor and a stage at one end, dressing rooms on either side of the stage, and a kitchen with a serving window. The upright piano at the other end of the room allowed for musical accompaniment.

Although the room was used for 4-H programs and various meetings during the year, there was something magical about it at Christmas with its twelve foot tree, rows of folding wooden chairs, and nervous children running around in their new holiday outfits, excited about the surprises we had for our parents and nervous about remembering our parts.

The Christmas program was the biggest event of the year. Right after Thanksgiving break, we started practicing plays and songs. Teachers sent home notes about costumes and pieces, which were memorized poems or recitations. Of course, schoolwork came first, but it was hard to focus at this exciting time of year.

We gave our parents invitations made in art class in the big room, but we welcomed the whole community. We drew names to buy gifts, keeping identities of giver and recipient secret. If we got the name of a good friend, we spent as much as fifty cents.

A typical Christmas program began with a first grade boy and girl reciting a greeting of welcome, and the rest of the first and second graders walking on stage, each carrying a letter to spell "W-E-L-C-O-M-E." This was followed by a musical chorus of "Frosty the Snowman" and a short play, such as "Dolly's Got the Flu," a dramatization about a sick little doll whose friends give their ideas of the diagnosis.

One year, when I had a piece in "Last Year's Doll," I wore a wig with stringy hair, an eye patch, and a dress big enough to put one arm inside. My mother stuffed the sleeve to look like a missing arm. The plays were always about families who had problems that were easily solved. The message of this particular play was, "Take care of this year's new doll."

During the Nativity scene, the best singer would sing "Silent Night." One year I played Mary, and my mother dyed a sheet light blue for my dress and lent me a white muslin dish towel for a veil. The boys wore bathrobes, and the angels wore white sheets and wings made of wire through gold garland. We softened the lighting with blue cellophane over light bulbs.

One year, rhythm band members on drums, triangles, sticks, blocks, and cymbals played and sang, "Here Comes Santa Claus." The finale featured the entire cast on stage in our best Christmas outfits singing "White Christmas," accompanied on the piano by Mrs. Riddle, the wife of a local farmer. The program concluded with the standing-room audience joining in.

As soon as we all got off the stage, we heard bells and "Ho Ho Ho." Santa gave each child a red open-weave net stocking filled with ribbon candy, peppermint canes, and nuts in the shell. Then, Santa distributed presents to the kids whose names we had drawn and also to the teachers. The children gave presents that had been made at school to their parents, and the school board gave an apple to everyone who attended. This was followed by a lunch of homemade buttered buns with dried beef or ham, decorated, homemade, Christmas cookies, and coffee and Kool-Aid, prepared by moms and served on paper plates. This program marked the beginning of Christmas vacation, so at the end of the evening, we made a big deal out of saying "See you next year!" though we'd probably see our friends before New Year's--either sledding on "Pike's Peak" or skating on the Straight River.

Every February, we took bus trips to the Cities to see the Shrine Circus or the factories of Fanny Farmer Candies, Land 'O Lakes, and Taystee Bread. In the spring, we played softball with other country schools like Steele Center and Lemond, taking turns playing at each other's schools as every school had a softball field. Since I was skinny, sickly, and unathletic, softball was not my favorite activity. I would get stuck in right field and pray no one would hit the ball to me. I think the first and second basemen played deep whenever I was out there. My dad promised me $1.00 for every fly ball I caught. The most I ever made was $2.00. The good part was that everybody played, both girls and boys, so it was a good time to meet cute boys or pretty girls at other schools.

Some very bright people came out of Hope school. Two became valedictorians at Owatonna High School. Dorothy Schiller and Sue Oldefendt and many of the rest of us went on to college and are doing well.   Judy Schuster was the first farm girl to be elected homecoming queen at Owatonna High School in 1958, and we Hope kids were especially proud. Hope School closed in 1971 when it consolidated with Owatonna. It was the last country school in Steele County and one of the last in Minnesota.

Margaret Steele Johnson is a parent educator in early childhood family education in suburban Minneapolis. She and her husband reside in Apple Valley, Minn., but she still believes the people in Hope are the best in the state.

Centennial Memories
Sharon McClintock Johnson

The most memorable event of my first ten years was the Owatonna Centennial celebration which occurred during May and June, 1954. The normally tranquil town was suddenly teeming with men in beards and women in sunbonnets. We bought wooden nickels, Centennial buttons, and best of all, we watched with interest the mysterious Kangaroo Court which was held in the bandstand in the town square.

One day during lunch hour, my friends and I walked downtown to watch the Kangaroo Court in action. It had been reported to be quite entertaining, and we just had to see for ourselves. The town's businessmen, in an effort to raise funds for the Centennial, charged each other with crimes such as being seen without their Centennial buttons, and because they had not grown beards, they could be fined. The townspeople watching the proceedings cheered, booed, or offered opinions as needed while each prisoner tried hopelessly to defend himself. It was a mystery to me why anyone would want to go through that, but the crowd, and especially World War I veterans who frequented the park, seemed to enjoy this strange form of entertainment.

I really wanted one of those centennial sunbonnets. However, I knew that saving anything out of my allowance of twenty-five cents per week, which I needed to pay for movies and candy, would be impossible. After offering my mom the opportunity to buy one for me and hearing her refusal, I gave up on that wish

Someone announced at church that people were needed to play parts in the Centennial pageant. My sister, Melissa, and I, drawn to theatrical events, excitedly accepted the offer to be part of this momentous event. We were to play pioneer girls in two scenes. The first was about a pioneer church, and we had singing parts; the second was about a hotel fire, and we had screaming parts. We had visions of very glamorous costumes. After all, we spent many Saturday afternoons at the theatre watching western movies where the women sashayed around in their beautiful long dresses and twirled their parasols.

When the costumes finally arrived, we were more than a little miffed. Not only were there no parasols, but all dresses were made of the most unattractive cotton prints we had ever seen. Unattractive costumes could not dampen our enthusiasm for being part of the big event, however.

The Centennial pageant, which would run four nights, was held in the grandstand at the county fairgrounds. A huge stage with a large canvas backdrop and platforms cascading down to the racetrack level had been constructed in front of the grandstand. Rehearsals were held for several nights, and it was thrilling for us to be there watching the older neighborhood kids and some adults we knew playing the parts of townspeople of the past.

The pageant began with the story of a Sioux Princess, Owatonna, who was brought to the town's mineral springs for a cure. Next came the arrival of the first settlers, a number of scenes which brought the story up to the present day, and then the grand finale number in which the stage and lower area were filled with the cast, horses, riders, and vintage vehicles. I enjoyed every performance and marveled at all the talent I never knew my neighbors and friends possessed.

The fourth and final night of the performance, midway through the spectacular, the sky darkened and an incredibly strong wind suddenly tore the stage backdrop curtain from bottom to top. This was tornado season, and everyone knew what that meant--get to a shelter fast. Frightened screams were heard, cast and crew scattered, and the grandstand quickly emptied. Melissa and I were behind the stage waiting for our next scene when the excitement began. As the older sister, it was my responsibility to make sure that we made it home safely, so we ran the only way I knew to get away from the danger, directly across the stage. I will never forget the awesome sight of the immense canvas backdrop flapping crazily in the wind with the stage crew struggling to control it.

Melissa and I held hands and ran quickly to get off the stage. My sister remembers that the ruffle on the bottom of her dress caught on something as we ran, and the torn dress caused another worry. We were supposed to take good care of those costumes. Although the wind remained strong and the sky stayed very dark, rain did not fall.

After Melissa and I had made our way out of the grandstand area, we stopped in the midst of the fleeing people hoping to find anybody familiar. Most of all, we wanted to find our dad. We knew he must be there but could not locate him. By now, it was as dark as night, and there were no familiar faces in sight. A car drove up and paused. Inside were an older man and woman who asked if we wanted a ride. As much as I wanted that ride, I had to tell them that my father had instructed us never to get into a car with people we didn't know. The strangers nodded in understanding. Then, the man asked our names, and upon hearing them, told us that he knew my dad and had sold him polio insurance. That was good enough for me; we would take that ride home!

When the car pulled up in front of our house, we were relieved and happy to see our parents. We were surprised, however, that they were not out looking for us. We discovered that they were not even aware of the excitement just a mile away. The storm, which was probably straight-line winds, had hit only the fairgrounds area. Much to my relief, my parents approved of my decision to accept the kindness of the insurance agent and his wife, and I felt proud that I had delivered my sister home safely.

Sharon McClintock Johnson is married and the mother of two daughters. She and her husband live in the Twin Cities area.

Pontoppidan
By Russell L. Christenson

In the place and time where I grew up, there was no such thing as an Identity Crises. You knew exactly who and what you were (and so did everyone else for miles around). You were Norwegian. You were a valued member of your family. Most likely, your name ended in "son" (as in Christenson, Johnson, Larson, Olson, Swenson, Hanson, Nelson or Tollefson). You lived in the community of Lemond, Minnesota, and you probably attended Pontoppidan Lutheran Church regularly: that meaning every Sunday unless your mother judged you to be so ill as to be truly at Death's Door.

We attended the Second Pontoppidan Lutheran Church. The first, built in 1977, had been razed, and the second one was built in 1922. The church lay exactly one mile north of our house as the crow would fly (if the crow wanted to go to church). Pontoppidan was a large, wood-frame building set up on a basement with a high foundation so that the church was taller than you would expect a one-story building to be.

It was painted white and had a tall roof and large stained-glass windows on either side of the building. Surrounding the church was a cemetery, where preceding generations rested in peace, except on the Fourth of July. A flight of concrete steps led up to the front doors which opened into a vestibule. One side of the vestibule stairs led up to the balcony. In the sanctuary, three rows of pews were separated by aisles. In front of the sanctuary was a large, ornately carved altar with a wooden pulpit to the right.

As with most churches I've attended, people tended to sit in the same section of the church every Sunday. I don't suppose anyone actually owned the pews, but sometimes they acted as though they did. An elderly couple made a habit of sitting on the right-hand end of the last pew in the center section. They were wealthy and well respected in the community.

One Sunday, when I was quite young, I decided to sit in their pew. They came in. The old man cleared his throat. I looked up at him and smiled but did not offer to move. He did not return my smile; instead, he and his wife turned on their heels, marched out of the church and went home. After that, I sat up in the balcony with my father.

Pontoppidan was more than a church. It was one of the two social centers of the community (the other being the schoolhouse). Once or twice a month, the Ladies' Aid Society would meet in the church basement, and, at various times, there would be church suppers attended by everyone in the congregation.

On the Fourth of July, a potluck dinner and an ice cream social followed the church service. The men set up a square area on the lawn, surrounded by tables made of sawhorses and planks. Inside the square, they had gallons of ice cream and cases of soda pop. They sold dishes of ice cream or ice cream cones and bottles of soda. More importantly, at least to the children, they sold rolls of caps for cap guns and packages of firecrackers. We set off firecrackers and played Cowboys and Indians or Cops and Robbers all over the cemetery. No one rested in peace that day.

In the autumn, the men and women of the church hosted a Lutefisk Supper. I think that Lutefisk is a Scandinavian word for fish that smells really bad. They cooked a hundred pounds of Lutefisk and served it with Lefse (a potato tortilla), mashed potatoes and gravy and all kinds of Scandinavian pastries. This supper usually coincided with pheasant season and drew people from as far away as Minneapolis and St. Paul. It was a good money-raiser, and it helped preserve the Scandinavian heritage for the young people of the community.

For several years, my parents were church janitors and my mother was the organist. On Saturday evenings, when we went to clean the church, my mother practiced hymns for the next day. I helped with cleaning and occasionally tried to play the organ.

On Sundays, I got to sit up in the balcony with my father. He rang the big bell a half dozen times to signal the beginning of church. When the service concluded, he rang the small bell to dismiss the congregation. In the beginning, I was only able to ring the small bell. If I tried to ring the big one, the rope lifted me off my feet as it recoiled toward the ceiling. Eventually, I grew into the task.

After the service was over, people gathered in the vestibule or on the steps outside to chat. The older parishioners often conversed in Norwegian.

"Gud Daggen" (Good Day) and "Ya, feena dag e dag" (Yes, fine day today). I knew these phrases and a few more, such as "Takkskidaha" (thank you), and "Mana Tusen Takks" (many thousand thanks). My mother also taught me to count to ten and to sing a little child's song in Norwegian. However, these were difficult to work into a conversation. Sometimes, by the end of the service, we were suffering from "Thresmach," a Norwegian word meaning "I have sat so long I can taste the wood."

When someone in the community died, a church official tolled the big bell. When the church bell began to ring at any time other than on Sunday, everyone in the community would stop what they were doing. Telephones rang as the word was passed from household to household about who had died, when the funeral would be held, and if possible, the details of the victim's demise. If school was in session, classes stopped, and we tried to figure out for whom the bell tolled. Who was that old? Who had been in poor health?

Funerals were social occasions in our community, just as they are in many other rural communities. Several years ago, I wrote my favorite poem after the funeral of my father-in-law, and I think it is pretty descriptive of a rural Minnesota funeral.

MORE TALK THAN TEARS

The church bell tolls them to their task.
One of their own has gone to rest.
No need for anyone to ask.
The town has given of its best.

He was a good old guy, you know.
Too bad he had to meet his end.
I guess it was his time to go,
And I was glad to call him friend.

They shuffle up the chapel aisle.
The Guest of Honor's in repose.
At first a tear and then a smile.
"The flow'rs are nice. Did we send those?"

The family gathers in the back
On shoulders, tender hands are laid.
Like settlers fending off attack.
"He's happy now. Don't be afraid."

They talk of cattle, corn and hogs.
"Lunch at the house, after the wake."
The price is up for good saw logs
(for them, the "staff of life" is cake).

A neighbor drains his coffee cup.
The breeze is up; it's turning cold.
He climbs into his pickup truck.
Each time one dies, it makes him old.

He gazes fields with practiced eye
A polka dances in his ear.
Too bad his old friend had to die
 Looks like we'll make some crops this year.

In our community, there was about as much certainty in death as there was in life. On the day of the funeral, nearly all activity in the community stopped, and every relative and friend attended. The preacher gave a short sermon. Then my mother or Mildred Larson played the organ while the congregation sang a couple of old familiar hymns.

At some point, Mildred played the organ while Clayton Paulson sang "I Come to the Garden Alone." Clayton had a high tenor voice, sometimes made a little thin and quavering by the emotion of bidding farewell to an old friend. There were no "Honorary Pallbearers" at a funeral in those days. The task was clear and specific: pick up exactly one-sixth of the weight of the casket and its occupant and then carry it from the church to the gravesite (also dug by friends). All work was done by hand.

When the preaching ended and the casket was lowered, everyone trouped into the church basement for sandwiches, cake and coffee. Initially, folks offered a few comments such as, "She was too young," or "He was pretty old," and "It was a blessing." Then the conversation turned to everything but any mention of the recently departed. "How are you? How are the kids?" "It's too dry." "It's too wet." "The crops don't look very good." "Looks like we could make a hundred bushels to the acre this year." "Well, gotta' go get the chores done." "Come by and see us sometime. Don't be such a stranger."

A funeral was a sort of bittersweet event. There was a bit of comfort in knowing that when it was our turn, we would be laid to rest among friends and our survivors would be cared for by people we had known all our lives. I don't know what they did with people who died in the winter. I suppose they could have stuck them in a snowbank, just as we did with packages of meat we brought home from the locker plant in Otisco.

I met Joan at Pontoppidan Lutheran Church. Her father had been born in the Lemond community, and when they moved back, she began attending Sunday School. We went through Sunday School and Confirmation Class together. For a number of years, we both sang in the church choir. I started out as an alto and eventually progressed to singing bass.

On Saturday evening, June 16, 1962,
You are invited to Pontoppidan Lutheran Church
Where Russell Lee Christenson And Joan Arlene Larson
Will be United in Holy Matrimony.
Rev. John Soley officiating

Joan and I were the last couple to be married in that church. A few weeks after our wedding, we got one of those dreaded midnight telephone calls. It was my cousin, Roger Stennes, calling to tell us that lightning had struck the bell tower and that the church was on fire. By the time we got to the church, only the framework was standing. It looked like a glowing skeleton of a building. Shortly after that, the flaming timbers crashed into the basement. The second Pontoppidan Lutheran Church had burned to the ground.

Russell Christianson is a speech pathologist in the Clinton, Missouri area. He is also a writer whose latest book is THE EYE OF THE SQUIRREL (Strong Stock Press, Deepwater, Missouri, 1999).

Y'all Come
By Maxine Peterson Sweatt

Moving into a new neighborhood is always difficult but in Minnesota, it can be a real challenge. How does a guy who has more than a hint of a Southern accent get acquainted with these clannish folks of German, Norwegian or Swedish ancestry? After moving from one cool and clannish community in southern Minnesota, we were a bit apprehensive about melding into a new neighborhood in rural Zumbro Falls. Just how does one make friends with these people?

My husband, who is from the South, had mentioned several times that we should cook a Brunswick stew sometime. This Minnesota kid had no idea what Brunswick stew was. His explanation included an open fire with a big pot filled with meat and vegetables that cooked all day. The host invites family, friends, and neighbors, and everybody has a good time. Maybe that would do the trick. But how would the Minnesota clans take to a pot of stew that simmered all day and was stirred with a paddle? Only one way to find out. We began to make plans for our stew party.

The cooking would be easy--just empty the freezer of last year's vegetables, put in some beef and chicken, dump in some dried butter beans and a couple bags of black-eyed peas. Of course, those would have to be imported from the South. My husband would stop at a store on his next run to New Orleans in the big rig.

Invitations would be the real problem. How do you invite people you don't know to your place? My husband had talked over-the-fence to the neighbors on each side. As they were working their fields, they had stopped to at least say Hello. Of course, they had asked him his name and commented, "You don't sound like you're from around here." He mentioned that his wife had graduated from Owatonna High School and Mankato State in order to let them know that one of us belonged here!

Our plans for the stew proceeded. Oh yeah, we'd better set a date. Let's make it Saturday week. When we extend the invitation, we'll let the guests suggest a time. After all, farm families have chores to do. We decided that if we told just the neighbors on each side of us, they could spread the word.

So off he went to see the two neighbors. When my husband told them of our plans, they said, "Sounds like it will be okay. It might be a good idea. After all, the neighbors don't get together much."

He then told them, "Now it is up to you to get the rest of the folks to the stew. Have folks come Saturday week." Of course, he had to tell them Saturday week meant the Saturday after next, and then he mentioned the date so they would have the right Saturday.

"What time will be good?"
"About three o'clock in the afternoon is fine."

As these two neighbors invited folks, they would say, "Come to the place just north of me, " and the other neighbors would say, "Come to the place just south of me." With those directions, everyone knew just where we lived and where to come on Saturday week. We guessed that people were beginning to check us out because cars drove past our place a little slower than usual.

The apprehension continued. How many are we cooking for? Will the 20-gallon cast iron pot be large enough, or will we have 15 gallons left? And we might as well make crackling cornbread to go with the stew. Give it the true Southern flare! After all, we have those two large cast iron fry pans that we might as well use.

Saturday week arrived at last. We rose at sunrise, got the cast iron pot out of the shed, and propped it in the shallow fire pit. We carried over some kindling, some bigger pieces of wood and a bag of charcoal. We started the fire and heated the pot. We raided the freezer of corn, tomatoes, butter beans, and the chicken and the beef we had readied earlier in the week. When we dumped everything into the pot, it was only half full! We dug some more stuff out of the freezer and went to the store and bought a couple gallon cans of mixed vegetables. We added water and beef and turkey stock, the three bags of black-eyed peas, and some dried beans. We let it heat up and then dumped in some salt, pepper, a tad of red pepper, and some sugar to smooth out the tomato flavor. After it started to cook and thicken, we added potatoes to top off the pot.

The smoke from the wood fire started filling the air. Folks in cars driving by were looking over to see what was going on in our yard. In typical Minnesota fashion, they gave just a quick glance since nobody wanted to be too obvious while observing others. We just kept on watching the fire and stirring the stew with the big flat paddle as we returned their subtle waves. After one o'clock, a couple of neighbors stopped to check out what was in the pot. They approved of what they saw and said they would be back in a little while.

By three o'clock, we had a yard full of cars and pickup trucks. Folks who wanted the option of getting out of our yard easily parked along the sides of the road. They started looking in the pot, talking to the folks they knew and nodding to the ones they didn't. We had set up lawn chairs, wood blocks, board planks, cement blocks and whatever else people could find to sit on or squat by. Folks who started to mill and mix commented on what a pretty day it was and wanted to find out how the farming was going. Soon the stew was thick and the cornbread was golden brown with a curled brown crust.

"Y'all come and get it."
The bravest approached the pot and said, "What kind of stew is that?"

My husband's reply was, "It's Must-Go-Stew. Everything in the freezer must go!"

Most replied, "Well, I never heard of that, but guess I'll try some." So with a big water dipper, we filled each bowl.

"Might as well add a piece of that cornbread to my plate."

After they got their food, everyone returned to their original sitting place. There was no point in changing things around at eating time. A few new folks wandered over to the stew pot, and the cycle was repeated.

About that time, we all heard tires screech and saw a deputy sheriff pulling into the yard. He jumped out of his car and dashed over to the stew pot. "I was just a cruising by and stopped to see what was happening." He had seen the pot simmering earlier on his rounds, and curiosity got the best of him. As he got back into his car, he said, "Save me some of that. I'll be back later."

Folks were coming back for more stew and cornbread. By this time, we had made three double batches of cornbread and were running out of stew. The deputy came back to join in as the comments continued.

"What's this in the cornbread?"

"Never had it this way before. We've always just thrown crackling out to the chickens. Guess we'll start saving them for cornbread."

"I've never had cornbread cooked in an iron fry pan--we always made it in a square baking pan."

"What kind of beans are these in this soup? They have a little black spot on them."

"Well, I ain't never heard of them"

We noticed one fella fishing out the black-eyed peas with his spoon and putting them in a pile on his plate. "What's the matter, don't you like them?"

"No, I'm just trying to get a bunch of them together by themselves so I can tell what they taste like!"

Folks ate and talked and mingled for the next two hours. By then it was chore time, so the crowd started thinning out. Everyone came by and politely told us that they had really enjoyed the stew and were glad they had come. We said we had enjoyed it too and asked them to stop by and see us again.

So how does one judge if a get-acquainted party has been a success? By how many neighbors have a party of their own! Before long, one neighbor had a machine shed party. He had just built a new machine shed that warranted a machine shed warming party. Another neighbor threw an Irish party so that nobody would ever forget that they were of Irish ancestry.

One family had a Libby's Party. Get a bunch of sweet corn out of the field, put it in a ten-gallon cream can, add a couple sticks of butter and fill the can with water to cover the corn. Put the lid on loosely and slip a tire over the can. Light the tire, and when it is burned up, the corn is ready. As you eat the corn, let the butter drip down your elbows. We'd never eaten better sweet corn.

The next year, we started the cycle of neighborhood parties all over again. We had a Sloppy Joe party. People came about one o'clock on a Sunday afternoon, and some folks stayed until after seven o'clock. A few stories, tales, and jokes they told were even on the rare side! This neighborhood had really warmed up!

That fall, we decided to move to my husband's beloved South. That was twenty-four years ago. To this day, our Minnesota neighbors are some of our dearest friends. Each year, as we exchange holiday greetings or occasionally return for a visit, they say they miss us and wish we would move back to Minnesota. They say nobody ever gets together anymore like they did when we lived in their neighborhood. So how does one get to know your Minnesota neighbors? Have a y'all come party!

Maxine Peterson Sweatt is a medical technologist who enjoys country living with her husband Ivan in Walnut Cove, NC.

Scrapbooks
By Kathy A. Megyeri

I wonder if all Minnesotans treasure their scrapbooks as I do. Now, at almost 60 years of age, I treasure my scrapbook more each day, especially now that I haven't parents to ask for dates, times, and specific memories. At least once a year, I drag them out of a dust-covered box in hopes that silver fish have not chewed through glue, pictures and pages. How else could I know that I only cost my parents $75 to be born? On a Madison, Wisconsin Methodist Hospital receipt dated 1943, I see that my mother spent ten days in the hospital with me at $6.00 a day, her maternity room fee was $5.00; another $5.00 for anesthesia, $1.00 for medicine, $2.00 for a dressing and $4.00 for a lab fee. I can't believe I was such a bargain.

I surprise myself at other memorabilia I thought important:

• A sixth grade paper invitation for a party hosted by the fifth grade mothers
• My seventh grade locker combination with a program card of classes and teachers from the first school day
• A piano recital program card listing my name under "Rondo in A Minor" by Mozart. Now, I can't even remember the song; I only remember the fear of forgetting it in front of family and friends.
• My confirmation photo
• My hometown's centennial poster
• A receipt for a hospital stay because I contracted mononucleosis in eleventh grade
•The Christmas card I sent in 1958 with a drawing of my Springer Spaniel that looks a lot like George W. Bush's dog Spot
• Girl Scout badges for excelling in ice skating, dancing and service. My commitment to service is all that remains.
• Local newspaper coverage of our troop's coat hanger collection. We sold good hangers to local dry cleaners and dress shops as a fundraiser.

• A science fair honorable mention for a project my dad completed on "How Water Runs Uphill." He made a small weeping willow that sucked water into its roots from a miniature fountain, but I typed the explanation of osmosis.

• A letter from my grandmother who lived in Los Angeles. In her beautiful handwriting, she wrote, "I suppose you have been working very hard in your school studies lately and I hope you will win out in every subject too. Yes, school days are the good old days that one never forgets, but it is connected with a lot of work, but what would life mean to us if we could not read or write?" Maybe that's one of the reasons why I was motivated to become an English teacher later on.

• A 1956 postcard from the Pasadena Rose Bowl Tournament because we attended it on our way to visit Grandmother.

• An eloquent news article on my senior year's homecoming game that reads: "Few, if any persons attending the game can recall a specific contest that found the capacity of the stadium so completely taxed. Overflow spectators knelt, sat on blankets, and squatted on all available cardboards, pop boxes, etc. The entire field was rimmed by a bowl-like throng. Even marginal gains during the time of play brought forth a response that filled the perfect football evening with boisterous sound."

• A 1956 and 1958 Red Pine Camp Award for Riding and Sportsmanship. I also won a camp archery diploma and a National Rifle Association Sharpshooter award. Now, I can barely fire a weapon or a bow, and I hate horses because I was thrown at camp. I remember that the only reason I won the Sportsmanship Award is because I voted for myself and broke a tie. I also remember being sent to that camp in Wisconsin because all the "rich girls" from my small Minnesota community attended each summer for eight weeks, probably to stay out of trouble over the summer, and my folks wanted me in good company. I used to brag about what an exclusive camp it was. Forty years later, I took my husband to see it. When he passed the wooden barracks with outdoor latrines, an ancient archery range and dilapidated horse barns, he commented that it looked more like a Nazi concentration camp. "Exclusiveness" changes its meaning after one is exposed to swankier events.

• A photo of my first sleep-over on a friend's living room floor in my baby doll pajamas

• A love note from a boyfriend:

February 25, 1959

Time: 10:15

Condition: Lonely and Blue

I'm home here with the radio on. You looked neat and pretty in church tonight. I wish I had been sitting there beside you up in front of the church. I'd like to go to church with you some Wednesday nite or on a Sunday for that matter too, but I like going to church better at night than in the daytime, unless you'd rather go on a Sunday. Do you think that your folks would let you go to the last Lent service with me? I wanted to talk to you longer tonight but Milton asked me to be sure and help put books and chairs away after the service so I thought that I'd better help. I suppose I'd better to go bed and get my mind all refreshed for school tomorrow. Oh, by the way, I hung the dice in my dad's truck, but he doesn't like them at all, so they'll probably be gone next week. Good-nite.

• A photo of the "new" group, the Everly Brothers who came to the Monterrey Ballroom outside town. My father was my date and couldn't understand what all the screaming was about. He also took me there to see Jerry Lee Lewis and thought the music was junk, but I haven't any photos of that event.

• A picture of my first car decorated for homecoming. It was a '36 Hupmobile we pasted with cut-out dots so we could dress up as clowns and throw candy at the spectators

•My high school choir teacher who made Teacher of the Year. In the photo, the choir is singing "Beautiful Savior," not allowed at today's school commencement because it's religious.

• A photo of my first date at age fourteen. He walked me to a Saturday matinee at the Roxy Theatre where we saw KING KONG, and he bought me a Mounds bar and Tootsie Rolls and then walked me home. I thought it was the perfect date. He's now a postal employee in Minneapolis.

• A photo of our high school prom held in the school gymnasium which was filled with pink plastic flamingos. The parents lined the walls of the gym taking photos of us, and a plastic fountain is in the middle of the floor spouting a small geyser.

• A photo of my wrist corsage that I tried to save in the refrigerator for weeks after the prom.

• A photo of me with my "helmet hair" that was teased and ratted. We all wore white pointed rhinestone cat-shaped eyeglasses, our boy-friend's class rings on chains around our necks, and knee ticklers that were the rage. Our sweaters were tight over our pointed bras, and the school's dress code required us to wear skirts. During the cold winters, we wore pants under those skirts, and one had to be a contortionist to change out of them in the halls in front of our lockers so the boys wouldn't see our underpants. We also wore bobby socks with our saddle shoes and frosted or streaked our hair in an attempt to look "cool."

• My high school commencement program

• My college freshman green beanie with a red button on top

• A March on Washington banner and button from August of 1963--my first summer in Washington, D.C. and a most momentous occasion because I heard Martin Luther King's "I Have a Dream" speech.

• A Goldwater poster from my first political rally on July 4, 1963 at the D.C. National Guard Armory. I didn't know that years later I would watch my husband in uniform parade on that floor and become activated for the '68 riots in D.C.

• My Nixon watch with flitting eyes and my Spiro Agnew handbag. My Nixon inaugural invitation went unused because my husband's National Guard unit was called up for traffic control, and I ended up staying home watching the events on TV.

Just last year, I updated my scrapbook by pasting in Happy Retirement cards after 34 years of teaching. Those snippets of paper and photos from the '50's and '60's substituted for the medals and trophies given kids today, but I hope mothers still encourage their kids to keep scrapbooks. I'll bet in Minnesota they do. With each passing year, I need that scrapbook more and more to reflect on a lifetime of truly significant memories.

The Country Hearth Motel
By Kathy A. Megyeri

After World War II, thousands of soldiers returned home in search of new careers and hopes of building a family and saving for retirement. My father was no different. He opened a Texaco station on Main Street in Owatonna, Minn. and worked days, nights, and weekends to make a life for his wife and two children. For just 29 cents per gallon of gas, he would wash car windows, check air pressure in the tires and the amount of oil in the engine, and wash all the manure off the bottoms of farm vehicles.

Dad worked long hours, so Mother cooked dinner and took it to him while my brother and I explored the station's garage and played with the tools. I learned to love the smell of gasoline and truly admired my dad's starched uniform with its Texaco Oil insignia. As automobile travel flourished in the late 1940's, Dad's business grew, and he eventually hired a night man so he could come home to eat dinner with the family.

At the same time, Josten's, the class ring and graduation announcement company headquartered in Owatonna, was expanding nationwide. Josten's President Dan Gainey respected my father's business acumen and convinced him to open a motel in town so the company's salesmen and representatives would have a comfortable, clean place to stay when they visited corporate headquarters. Although Dad had no experience in offering overnight lodging, he was willing to try.

The motel concept was new and exciting. Previously, most travelers rented cabin courts and hotels, but the idea of parking your car by your room, conveniently unloading your luggage, and being attended to by a person in a front office gave rise to a new term: motoring + hotel gave us "motel."

So, in the early '50's, Dad and Mother opened the Modern Aire Motel on Highway #14. The motel was literally my home, even after Interstate #35 diverted traffic and my parents opened their second motel across town, The Country Hearth. At both places, Dad and Mother were quite successful because they worked 24 hours a day, 7 days a week, 52 weeks a year. I remember only one family vacation in my entire childhood and that was to Wisconsin Dells for a four-day weekend. Mom and Dad then hired motel "sitters," an English couple who assured themselves a good night's sleep by turning on the "No Vacancy" sign and going to bed, something my parents would never think of doing. For years, Dad got up, slipped on his bathrobe and answered the door at all hours of the night to wait on customers unless all rooms were legitimately full.

My mother loved her guests. Most days, she would bake her tasty chocolate chip cookies and set them on the motel's front desk for the salesmen who would check-in about four or five o'clock each day. She knew each by name, inquired of their families and pets, and remembered something special about each. Newlyweds and anniversary couples could count on some of those cookies in their rooms along with a bottle of wine or champagne. It made for terrific repeat business.

Some customers returned even after they retired to introduce their children to Mom and Dad, and other customers stopped yearly on their way to their favorite vacation spots in northern Minnesota, usually on some lake, so they, too, became familiar faces. Mother cleaned the rooms each morning right along with the two long-time cleaning girls. They, too, enjoyed her cookies at coffee break mid-morning.

At noon, Mother would wash the mounds of towels and sheets from the twenty-six motel rooms. I remember her ironing the pillow cases by running them through a huge machine that held a massive roller which was heated to well over 200 degrees.

Dad was the handyman, security guard, and bathroom cleaner. They worked as an inseparable team. When long-distance truckers came in mid-day for their mandatory sleep time, Mother was careful to give them a quiet, back room, but she always remembered the wake-up call they requested so they could get back on the road. Even when the new chain called Holiday Inn came to town, Mom and Dad's customers stayed with them for that "personal and tender loving care" they got no where else. How they had time to raise my brother and me is still a mystery to us both.

Living in a motel was quite fun. We each had our own rooms that looked to outsiders like regular motel rooms. My parents' little apartment behind the front office consisted of a living room, kitchen, and bedroom, so it was convenient for them to be there all the time. Each motel room was decorated like a miniature family room from the '50's with a wall-mounted TV, single desk, telephone, plush red carpet and clean, chenille bedspread. Mother found a caner in Waseca who recaned antique rocking chairs for the rooms, and she washed the bedspreads weekly to get rid of cigarette smoke. In those days, no such luxury as a non-smoking room existed.

Dad ran the Texaco station in front of the motel as well, so when he finished cleaning bathrooms at the motel, he scrubbed the gas station ones too and never complained. No dirty job was beneath him, and there always seemed to be dirty jobs.

I remember my parents dreading two types of customers: Harley Davidson motorcycle groups on their way each summer to Sturgis for the annual rally, and ball players who came to town for tournaments. Motorcycle owners thought nothing of rolling their huge touring bikes across the room's new plush carpet so they could completely overhaul the engine, while ball players, both softball and baseball, brought six-packs and kegs of beer into the rooms and got so drunk that they threw up just about anywhere.

I remember one particular kitten-ball player, as he was called, who did not make it to his room to relieve himself He peed in a corner in front of the outside steps that led to his second floor room. My father caught him, grabbed him by the neck, and after forcing his nose into his own urine, handed him a rag and made him clean it up. I thought the offender lucky that my father didn't hurt him more, but Dad prided himself on running a "clean, well-lighted place," as Hemingway wrote.

My parents finally ended up turning bikers and ball players away. It wasn't worth the $7.50 a day room rate, and that's what they charged in the early '50's.

Their favorite customers were those good-looking Josten's salesmen--all young, blond, polite and clean-cut--and the Funk's Seed men who came to detassle corn and experiment with new varieties of seed. I can remember one particular morning when my father was stripping the sheets off the beds before the cleaning girls arrived. That was always his first job each morning because the armloads of laundry got too heavy for the cleaning girls to carry to the laundry room.

But one morning, Dad inadvertently forgot to check to see if the room had been vacated, and he walked in on a most beautiful woman who sat naked at the desk brushing her long blonde hair while her husband showered in the bathroom. Dad profusely apologized and quickly shut the door, but he never stopped telling the story of one of the most beautiful women he had ever seen naked.

Across the highway and on the other side of Alexander's Lumber Company, the town dump was located. It attracted bats. Periodically, they would alight on the motel's eves and rafters. Some customers opened their room doors and became hysterical when they looked up to find a bat sleeping on the eves, so Dad invented a bat catcher, which he used almost daily. He cleverly nailed half a tennis ball to a long pole and sucked the bat into the ball like a plunger to carry it elsewhere and release it. Of course the reason we had so few mosquitoes and insect pests around the motel was because of the bats, but few customers appreciated them.

Probably the most difficult event for both my parents occurred the year following the fall of Saigon. A Viet Nam veteran checked into a room and soon after, my parents heard an awful explosion. The veteran had lain on the bed, placed a shotgun between his legs with the barrel in his mouth, and pulled the trigger. You can imagine the scene when they both entered to investigate. They called emergency crews, the mortician and medical examiner. The clean-up took most of the day. Walls had to be washed and repainted, bedding destroyed, and carpet replaced. The bereaved parents refused to pay for the damages, even after Mom and Dad returned the veteran's suitcase. That traumatic event left my parents shaken for months.

Winters were dreadful. My father plowed snow with a tractor to make sure the customers could get to their cars from their rooms, and he jump-started more vehicles than he cares to remember.

Minnesota summers are awfully hot, and although the motel did not have a pool, the Country Kitchen Restaurant next door served great ice cream, and Mother always had lemonade in the front office. She even planted flowers in urns in front of each room door to make the place a little homier.

What made the motel special for me was that I always had a place to bring my college friends to. Sleeping in your own motel room after dorm life was a special treat, so my roommates loved to come home with me for weekends.

Mom and Pop motels have gone by the wayside, and after my parents reached their mid-sixties, they too, decided to retire to their own real home on the other side of town. Indians from India now run the Country Hearth, along with many other small Minnesota motels. When I returned to Owatonna last summer, I stayed in the room that was my bedroom for years. It seemed small, featureless, and only the tile on the bathroom floor was the same.

The antique rockers were gone, probably all stolen by those who realized their value. The original hand-painted art work that once graced the walls had been replaced by prints of garish flowers. The bedspread smelled like smoke, although I had requested a no-smoking unit, and some kid's mountain bike was parked outside my door.

I hated the place, probably because somewhere in my mind, I could still smell my mother's chocolate chip cookies, could hear my dad bringing extra towels to a room nearby, and knew that no one in the front office either knew or cared about me. The only question the Indian woman in a sari asked was, "How do you want to pay for this?" Even the ice machine was broken, and I knew if I ever returned to town, I would stay at the newly refurbished Holiday Inn up the road with its bar, pool, and restaurant. You can't go back home again, especially if the motel room you used to call your bedroom has a cigarette burn on the bathtub and an old candy wrapper under the bed.

The Most Perfect Minnesota Mother
By Kathy A. Megyeri

I was 53 years old before I discovered my mother was once a runner-up in an Owatonna, Minn. beauty pageant. A couple of years ago, in a retrospective about the events of 65 years ago, my hometown newspaper profiled the pageant held at the movie theatre and its winner, still alive at that time and still quite gorgeous at age 83. There, in a sidebar, was a line about the pageant's two runners-up, and I read the name over and over: Mabel Bartsch, my mother's maiden name. She never mentioned it, never bragged of it, and there exists no photo of her in her pageant gown. If my high school girlfriend hadn't sent me the article, I never would have known. Dad always said, "You know, your mother was a real beauty," and that much we knew, but he never told me more.

After seeing the article, I looked for the first time at the life my mother enjoyed before me. With the self-centeredness of all children, I never really focused on her days before I became part of her life. Her own family moved to town after eking out a living as farmers, and her mother cleaned houses and washed walls for 25 cents a day. As the youngest of six children, my mother had to financially help the others, so following high school, she clerked at J.C. Penney's. She met my father in the church choir. He clerked at Leuthold's-St. Clair clothing store so they made quite a dapper couple.

When Dad joined the Air Force in 1941, mother gave up whatever career she might have pursued to follow him from one Air Force base to another. While Dad was stationed at Truex Field in Madison, Wisconsin, I was born. After the war, we returned to Owatonna where Dad went into business and Mother became the quintessential homemaker. Shortly thereafter, my brother was born, and when my parents opened up a motel and gas station complex on the main highway, they truly became business partners.

Mother totally devoted herself to raising both of us, juggled her work and mothering responsibilities, and never spoke of a career in fashion, modeling, or merchandising that she might have pursued. She made us believe we were enough for her, and the roles of wife, mother and businesswoman were her awards. She relished relationships with neighbors, relatives, and friends. She baked cookies and bars for St. John's Lutheran Church functions. She made homemade vegetable soup for elderly neighbors and sick relatives. She was a "people person" so she truly cared who was elected to the city council, whose kids made the honor roll, and who was admitted to or released from the hospital.

She religiously pasted Green Stamps in her redemption book and prided herself on knowing each clerk's name at Piggly Wiggly, the First National Bank, and Cashman's Seed Store. She loved plants, so our home was always filled with ferns, potted violets, and geraniums in window boxes. Though not a voracious reader, she assiduously studied the church bulletin to see who gave the most money to last Sunday's collection plate. She never missed reading "Hints to Heloise" or "Dear Abby" columns in the daily paper after she studied the obituaries, weddings, and misdemeanor charges that were posted there.

Dad obtained the first little black and white TV in the neighborhood, so Mom insisted we sit as a family to watch "I Love Lucy" and the "Ed Sullivan" show while she made us popcorn. Although Lutheran, she was especially kind to missionaries of all sects. I would frequently come home from school to see her surreptitiously give quarters to the Seventh Day Adventists as they handed her a magazine or to the Mormons as she kindly ushered them out the front door.

She was frugal but oh, so generous with us kids. I think I was the only high school senior who had both a class ring and a class pin because Mother, who never had either herself, splurged on me. Evenings, she cross-stitched aprons, embroidered pillowcases, and tatted handkerchief borders. The kitchen was her private domain.

We always enjoyed three course dinners, and not a day passed when we didn't devour fresh chocolate chip cookies, fruit pies, or baked bars after school. Sunday mornings, we dressed up for church, sat together as a family in the same pew and then drove to St. John's Lutheran Cemetery so we could water the plants on relatives' graves. Then, we drove home to dinner and usually spent Sunday afternoons driving to Red Wing in our red Ford convertible so my brother could climb in the caves on the bluffs overlooking the town. On the way home, Mom and Dad treated us to Dilly Bars at the Diary Queen. Our existence was simple and idyllic.

But life in a Midwestern small town had a dark side as well, according to Val Farmer, a Fargo columnist. If a person deviated too far from local wisdom, became too difficult or violated community norms, the townsfolk were disturbed. There was some danger in being too unique, too flawed, too self-centered or in distinguishing oneself too much. The connection people had with one another made them vulnerable to comparison, gossip, and control by public opinion and people pleasing. Thus, our minister's wife was criticized when she sat in the front pew dressed in a wide-brimmed hat and the latest fashion--what was she trying to do? Show off? When Cadillac unveiled a new sporty model, and Dad bought Mother one as a gift, she kept it only a year because the neighbors would think "we were putting on airs." Social approval meant everything. People worried about their image and appearance, which was maintained by the family's tight control. We hid our real feelings behind masks of happiness and success, and our behavior was governed by the following rules:

"We don't hang out our dirty linen."
"Real men don't cry."
"Don't make waves."
"You've made your bed, and now you have to lie on it."
"If you fall off, you get right back on."
"We get along with everyone."
"Don't blow your own horn."
And above all, "WHAT WILL THE NEIGHBORS THINK?"
"A parking ticket? What will the neighbors think?"

"I can't drive that Cadillac--what will the neighbors think?"

"My brother and his wife are having marital problems. I hope they don't air their problems publicly. What will the neighbors think?"

"We have to rake the lawn today. If we don't, what will the neighbors think?"

"We have to visit your grandmother at the nursing home this Sunday too, or what will the neighbors think?"

So my mother did her best to fit in with perceived community norms that contributed to the myth that life was wonderful, the kids were all above-average, and most of all, we could "cope." Fearful of being exposed as inferior in this "looking good" community, Mother was a worrier and workaholic. Idleness was a sin, so she was never idle. No other mother sewed printed name tags on all camp clothes, including underwear. No other mother cleaned her whole house and then helped the cleaning girls clean 28 rooms at the motel. No other woman baked brownies and took them to the local jewelry store owner whose wife was hospitalized. And Mom worried about the smallest detail; the traffic around the Cities (Minneapolis) would be bad, so we better leave real early. With that polio scare, the kids better not swim in the gravel pit this summer. We'd better turn around and go back to check that the oven is turned off. Let's hurry and take the wash in because it looks like rain. There might be more people than expected at the Mother-Daughter church banquet, so let's make some more bars, just in case. Extra worry would stave off any calamity.

Thus, my mother was the most perfect Minnesota mother. She was beautiful, competent, hard working, devoted to her husband and children, thoughtful, and a good churchgoer. Testimony to her contributions were in evidence at her funeral. Over 150 people came to pay tribute to a woman who couldn't be matched in personifying Minnesota's balanced lifestyle, sense of community, and rich and rewarding relationships with friends, neighbors and relatives. She left such a rich legacy that her tombstone reads, "Mabel Bartsch Wilker, Giving, Caring, Loving." Whenever I want to share a Minnesota Moment with her, I whip up a batch of her favorite bars, and then I know she's with me in spirit:

Good Cookie Bars

From the Kitchen of Mabel Bartsch Wilker

1 1/4	cup white sugar
3/4	cup brown sugar
2	cups flour
1/2	cup soft butter
1/2	cup flaked coconut
1/2	cup chopped walnuts

1 egg well-beaten
1/2 tsp. salt
1 tsp. baking powder
1 cup buttermilk
1 tsp. vanilla

Combine sugars, flour and butter. Cut into fine crumbs. Take 2 cups mixture out and into this, mix the coconut and nuts. Press into 8x11 pan and set aside. Be sure to use this size of pan. Mix all other ingredients together and spread over what is in pan. Bake at 350 degrees for 40 to 45 minutes. Put on icing or let cool and sprinkle with powdered sugar. Enjoy!

Today I Cried at Elvis' Grave
By Kathy A. Megyeri

The year 2000 was momentous for me in two ways. One, I retired from high school teaching after 34 years, and two, I finally went to Memphis to see Graceland, a lifelong dream of mine, particularly after following news of its owner for so many years. For those of us who grew up in Minnesota in the 50's, Elvis and Graceland were synonymous with bobby socks, big hair, the Ed Sullivan show, and rock 'n roll, our music. It was only last year, after strolling through Graceland's kitchen, recording studio, offices, pistol range, and the "jungle room" that I realized why, after the White House, Graceland is the most visited residence in the United States. Graceland affects visitors in a most profound way, and I'd like to share my experience.

December 18th was my 30th wedding anniversary, and I knew my husband would probably not remember it (true) or would not think of anything special to do on that date (also true), so I booked an inexpensive AirTran flight to Memphis for the weekend, and we stayed at the Adams Mark Hotel off Poplar Street. Unfortunately, the weather that weekend was cold and windy with an ice storm that almost paralyzed the city. Schools were closed and accidents were reported on Highway #240. But months ago, I had reserved two tickets for Monday morning on the first tour, and I was determined we would be there on time.

We got up early, had breakfast in the hotel, and skidded our way into Graceland's parking lot at 8:45. My husband said, "On a day like this, no one will be here," and he was almost right. There were only the workers so our rented Toyota was the first in the parking lot. Some of the attendants were even tardy, wheeling out the portable headsets and speakers that one wears while touring the mansion. Unfortunately, I have only an old camera with flash attachment, and since no flashes are allowed on the tour, I surreptitiously took photos of the beautiful holiday decorations that were just the way Elvis enjoyed them. Because there were so few tourists, we could take our time as we leisurely strolled from room to room listening to the accompanying tape.

An almost reverent hush falls over visitors as they walk silently through the mansion, and a young man beside me took copious notes on the contents of each room. What surprised my ambivalent husband the most was the trophy room. I don't think he ever realized the extent of Elvis' music sales. But while he wandered ahead of me, I was able to soak in each exhibit and reflect on why this visit was so meaningful to me, especially the Memorial Garden, the last stop on the tour.

While I stood alone over Elvis' grave, took photos, silently wept, and reflected on both our lives, a caretaker in a blue parka came to whisk away wilting wreaths and replace them with new arrivals, one even from Belgium. It made for a most fitting moment of reflection.

I think I was particularly moved because I was crying not only for the sad death of Elvis, but for my own lost youth in Minnesota. I went through high school knowing every song lyric and every movie that Elvis appeared in. In fact, my best friend admitted to me that her sexual awakening occurred when Elvis sang, "I Want You, I Need You, I Love You."

His comings and goings to and from Graceland were dutifully noted, and we all envied Priscilla who moved into Graceland and continued going to high school. How could any teenager be so lucky?

I was married in Dec. of 1970, when Elvis' career was almost at its peak. Two days after my wedding, Elvis met with President Nixon at the White House and surprised him with a hug. I even have a magnet of that famous picture of the "King and the Prez" on my refrigerator door.   At that meeting, Elvis gave Nixon an antique gun, and Nixon gave Elvis a genuine narcotics agent badge, which is on view at Graceland among his medals and badges.

I was saddened to learn just recently that Elvis had not planned that visit, but that he suddenly decided to visit Nixon after a quick trip to Los Angeles and back to Washington by plane.

Unannounced, he appeared at the gates of the White House where guards let him in. At that time, his friends and acquaintances already knew of his misuse of pills and drugs.

In 1970, I had already taught for five years in some obscure high school in Maryland and was concerned mostly with putting my husband through law school and grading students' papers. Yet, foremost in the media was this star at the peak of his career who was experiencing both fame and fortune, truly the American dream come true. Elvis had lost his mother two years earlier, and although I hadn't yet lost my mother, she was later to die in much the same way as Elvis--found on the bathroom floor, dead of heart failure.

When I looked at the artifacts that Col. Tom Parker had encouraged Elvis to market, I realized that my own closet contained many of them, particularly a favorite scrapbook with Elvis on the cover. Even though I was so busy in the early 1970's with husband and career, I still followed every occurrence in Elvis' life, many of which were photographed at Graceland. That year Elvis also had a string of big hits: "Don't Cry, Daddy," "Kentucky Rain," "The Wonder of You," and "You Don't Have to Say You Love Me." Elvis' album "On Stage" was released in February of 1970 and reached #13 on the charts.

There were other personal reasons I felt so connected to this star. I love jewelry, big jewelry, and I admire a man who can wear large pieces with confidence as Elvis did. His wide belts, his Indian pieces, his rings, his embroidered and sequined outfits with high collars and wrap-around sunglasses are still imitated and copied by Elvis "would-be's" today. Film director Hal Wallis reflected that when he met Elvis, he was surprised that Elvis had prepared for his audition by memorizing General McCarthy's Farewell speech. I, too, as a teacher had to be prepared every day for my classes or the students would not respect me or even listen to the lessons. Director Wallis also recalled that Elvis was concerned at his audition that he would have to smile in the movies, and Elvis knew that Marlon Brando, Sal Mineo, and James Dean seldom smiled in films. I, too, remember that as a young teacher, I was told not to smile the first month of school because it helped establish discipline in the classroom by conveying the impression to students that there would be no "fooling around."

Fellow actor Walter Matthau remembered Elvis' professionalism on the movie set of KING CREOLE. He said, "He was very intelligent....elegant, sedate, refined and sophisticated." I, too, remembered that one of my goals as a teacher was to have my students and colleagues think of me as competent and professional.

Television host Ed Sullivan commented on the polite gentlemanliness of Elvis. On one of the early shows, Sullivan said, "This is a real decent, fine boy." I, too, valued politeness and reverence for my elders. Even when the principals for whom I worked were younger than I, I still addressed them as "Mr." because their title meant a superior position, and I had been taught to revere that.

Elvis' daughter, Lisa Marie, recalled that he was a voracious reader, especially of philosophy and spiritual works, and that he often recorded his reactions to passages in the margins, as evidenced in the books open on his desk. I, too, pencil in reactions and questions in the margins of books I read.

Elvis was noted for his generosity, not only to friends but to causes. For some reason, it is not widely known that Elvis raised $65,000 to help build the U.S.S. Arizona Memorial, a World War II monument. I, too, have tried to be generous with my time and gifts, especially to promote students and help them publish their outstanding written pieces.

While some laugh and criticize Elvis' "jungle room," I loved the carved ram's head on the hardwood coffee table, the antlers, and the animal fur pillow on those Louis XV style chairs in red leather in the billiard room. In fact, I have some fur pillows and antlers in my own home, and only recently did we remove old shag carpeting from our TV room. Those were accoutrements of the '70's and certainly weren't considered "tacky" back then.

At my last class reunion, we were encouraged to dress in '50's style clothes and bring artifacts that we treasured. Out of a class of 400, I was the only one to borrow cat-eye glasses, bee-hive my hair like Priscilla's wedding photo, wear my Elvis t-shirt and jewelry, bring my Elvis scrapbook, and drag in the plaster bust of Elvis that I have sitting on my mantel. In that garb, I gave the keynote speech of the evening in which I compared my innocent, wonderful high school days in the small Minnesota town of Owatonna to suburban high school students of today. In my speech, I read the only address Elvis wrote, which he delivered to the Jaycees when he won his "One of the Ten Outstanding Young Men of the Nation" Award in 1970. His message signified the attainment of the American Dream, and for my classmates, it recognized the power of music in our lives:

"When I was a child, ladies and gentlemen, I was a dreamer. I read comic books, and I was the hero of the comic book. I saw movies, and I was the hero in the movie. So every dream I ever dreamed has come true a hundred times...I learned very early in life that: 'Without a song, the day would never end; without a song, a man ain't got a friend; without a song, the road would never bend; without a song.' So I keep singing a song. Good night. Thank you."

Years later when I met former President Jimmy Carter at a book signing, he looked surprised when I thanked him for the White House statement that marked Elvis' death on August 16, 1977. I remembered the lines that Carter wrote: "Elvis Presley's death deprives our country of a part of itself. He was unique, irreplaceable…..and he was a symbol to people the world over of the vitality, rebelliousness and good humor of this country."

I thought those three adjectives so fitting for Elvis and so remarkable coming from a President. These are the memories that converged upon me as I stood over Elvis' grave on my wedding anniversary. I think that many of my fellow Minnesota classmates were affected in much the same way. Elvis deserved my tears, and because of my memories and Elvis' impact, I was changed in ways that made me who I am today. Elvis, thank you, thank you very much.

50 Remembrances of Minnesota Life in the 50's
by Kathy A Megyeri

Garrison Keillor once wrote that all he does is say the words: "cornfield and Mother and algebra and Chevy pickup and cold beer and Sunday morning and rhubarb and loneliness, and other people put pictures to them." For me, other lists come to mind concerning what I remember most about Minnesota and my teen years in Owatonna during the '50's.

1. Attending beer parties at Mineral Springs Park. Actually, they were more like "root beer" blasts while we practiced smoking Camels to look really cool, fashionable, and macho

2. Going to Halloween dances, after-game mixers, and sock hops at the Armory

3. Surviving girls' gym classes wearing ugly blue bloomers and white blouses and playing 45 minutes of basketball that could have been played by two (Barb and Wilma, the class's tallest girls)

4. Practicing OUR TOWN, which seemed to be the yearly school play

5. Celebrating graduation--a class that now consists of four farmers, two doctors, one attorney, one mayor, one principal, thirteen teachers, sixteen self-employed persons, three ministers, three engineers, one stock-broker, 306 children and 25 grandchildren.

6. Driving to the A&W Root Beer stand to meet others, oogle the roller skating carhops, and order hamburgers, brown cows and chicken-in-the-basket over the loud-speaker

7. Using the compass and protractor for geometry class and then sticking one another in the rear between classes with the protractor's sharp end

8. Chatting during the summer on the outside porch while swatting our exposed body parts to kill mosquitoes; the bug zapper came much later

9. Enduring three short seasons and an interminably long fourth season of winter

10. Smelling the scent of Lilacs and Lilies of the Valley each spring

11. Complaining that dancing and card playing were not allowed at Luther League parties, but appreciating that hayrides and bowling parties were sanctioned by the minister as "appropriate fun."

12. Using closets for clothes; they were not something you "came out of"

13. Holding rabbits at Easter that were not VW's. One Easter, we coerced Dad into buying us two baby chicks. They grew so big we eventually had to give them to a nearby farm.

14. Treasuring a "meaningful relationship" meant getting along with your cousin

15. Valuing "time-sharing" meant hours spent with relatives at a family reunion and hating every minute of talking with those old people I barely knew

16. Knowing that anything "Made in Japan" usually meant junk

17. "Making out" meant how you did on your last exam

18. Mowing "grass." Who would know it could be inhaled?

19. Putting peanuts in my "Coke" (called "pop") at Woolworth's soda fountain

20. Admiring "Aides" who were helpers in the principal's office. Who would ever think "Aids" would later identify the most dreaded disease known to man?

21. Realizing that people married first and then lived together. If a girl got pregnant, she just disappeared from high school for a few months to "visit family"

22. Admiring "Designer jeans" that cost $2.99 at J. C. Penney's

23. Fasting during Lent meant giving up chocolate for a couple of days

24. Calling someone literate meant they were well read; certainly not "computer literate" because "software" wasn't a word

25. Being totally ignorant of pizza, instant coffee, radar, laser beams, computer dating, dual marriages, nursing homes, FM, guys with earrings, electric typewriters, yogurt, day care, group therapy, air conditioners, McDonald's, clothes dryers, and Valium because they weren't around yet either

26. Knowing that "outer space" meant only the back of the

Roxy Theatre in the balcony, the best place for "necking"

27. Enjoying the fact that a used Chevy Coup was $600, gas was 24 cents a gallon, and an ice cream cone, a Pepsi and a phone call were 5 cents.

28. Singing "Beautiful Savior" with the high school chorus. I could never get through it without my eyes misting over.

29. Loving slumber parties where we danced to 45-rpm records in someone's living room and slept on blankets tossed on the floor after gossiping till the wee hours of the morning.

30. Getting to know the real oddities in my high school who were the foreign exchange students--one from France and the other from Ecuador.

31. Driving to Rochester every other Monday afternoon to have the braces on my teeth tightened because there were no orthodontists in Owatonna.

32. Perusing the Owatonna Daily People's Press to see how many new polio cases were diagnosed. Fear of polio curtailed summer activities and mandated early afternoon naps.

33. Hating my weekly piano lessons and begging my dad to let me quit, but he was determined I should be as musical as he was for he played trumpet in the community band and always wanted us to play duets at the old folks' home. The refrain, "Someday you'll thank me for these music lessons" proved false. I still think the lessons were a waste of time and money.

34. Being forbidden to go to the drive-in movie theatre with a boy. Later after meeting my husband-to-be, I was stuffed in the trunk of his '40 Dodge to save the $2.50 admission fee at the drive-in movie gate. During the "coming attractions," I crawled out of the trunk and into the front seat and then proceeded to the snack booth for a big tub of popcorn. Eating was just as much fun as necking, I thought. Food was a secondary expense. It never cost more than the price of a ticket.

35. Smelling blue ditto papers that teachers passed out

36. Remembering the kid next to me in Social Studies who passed gas, and while the rest of us giggled, the oblivious teacher kept lecturing on the state constitution.

37. Loving Bill Holden, my 10th grade English teacher who

wrote "good" on my little autobiography. In fact, I received so much satisfaction out of writing for his class that I became an English teacher like him. Today, I don't know whether to thank him or blame him.

38. Dreading the time when your parents' friends noticed a discrepancy between your expected behavior and your actual behavior because then they phoned your parents and ratted on you.

39. Anticipating the coming of trampoline centers because they finally put up one at the A&W Root Beer stand, and kids waited in line to try it.

40. Getting punished with the belt. I once sneaked the car over to Faribault after being forbidden to take it outside Owatonna's city limits, and I got the belt. It didn't matter that I was 17--(the term "parental cruelty" did not exist.)

41. Shoveling snow, wearing Kickerinos, and begging to be driven to school instead of walking through drifts. School was never cancelled because of weather conditions.

42. Listening to radio, especially WDGY, Cedric Adams on WCCO, Ed Viehman, Arthur Godfrey, Don McNeil's breakfast club, and Todd Hale's Community Bulletin Board for births, engagements, weddings, and death announcements.

43. Anticipating Christmas because it meant heading to Dayton's in Minneapolis to stand in line for hours to see Santa. Funny how Dayton's was such a part of my life. I remember getting my first "curse" in the ladies' room at Dayton's, and my mother rushed out before she bought the required Kotex and rubber lined panties to tell Dad who was waiting for us. I was mortified and thought surely that Dayton's would announce the arrival of my blossoming womanhood on their intercom system.

44. Crying through "Lassie Come Home" and "Old Yeller" at the movie theatre which first featured an old piano player and then those black and white newsreels.

45. Working at the local jewelry store after school polishing silver, registering bridal selections and selling the local farmers just about anything on Christmas Eve

46. Reading in the Daily People's Press that another farmer's elevator worker had fallen to his death in the grain bin

47. Taking for granted the Louis Sullivan designed bank building facing the town square that people from all over the world came to photograph

48. Driving my '36 Hupmobile to school and decorating it for the Homecoming parade. Dad found that car and refurbished it for me for my senior year in high school. With its "suicide doors," chrome front grille, velvet seats, and bright yellow exterior, I thought it a Rolls Royce. The only drawback was that I had to take my younger brother everywhere, and I hated being seen with that little creep.

49. Tormenting the kids in the "Opportunity Room" at school. Now they are called "Developmentally Challenged," receive federal funding, and each is assigned an instructional assistant.

50. Losing my innocent perspective about the safety of small town life after learning about Ed Gein, Wisconsin's mass murderer, who committed atrocities north of Plainfield, Wisconsin, near my summer camp. Gein shattered my complacency and my certainty that weird and disturbed people lived somewhere else, not in my back yard. I had always been sure of that.

Life in the Past Participle and the Slow Lane
By Graham Frear

What seest thou else
In the dark backward and abyss of time.
Shakespeare-RICHARD III

Rolling farm land broken with woods of great white oaks and elms near the famous creek Minnehaha, immortalized by Longfellow, is now covered with two and three garage suburban ramblers and blacktopped driveways lined with newly planted spruce, lilac, birch clumps and magnolias. Once rich cropland is now a closely cropped, power-mower wasteland without goldenrod, oxeye or cattails hiding ring-winged blackbird nests.

Minnehaha Creek still runs, less exuberantly, from Lake Minnetonka to its famous falls above the Mississippi through densely packed suburbs of Hopkins, St. Louis Park and Edina, past country clubs and shopping malls with parking lots as large as the old Minneapolis airport. Once bucolic, narrow roads swarm with SUV's, 4x4's and glossy pickups driven by well-coiffed women in Jordache jeans and Kaffe Fassett hand-knit sweaters. Their pickups are stuffed with grocery bags or black plastic ones crammed with oak and elm leaves from pristine lawns.

Minnetonka Mills in my salad days was a sparsely populated village surrounded by small farms, a few regal houses near the long abandoned M and L Street right-of-way and Minnetonka Boulevard passing the village grocery, and a filling station. Ernie's garage was redolent with spilled gas, engine oil and cigarette butts in the ash around the pot-bellied wood stove; outback, a melange of old engine blocks, rusted mufflers and spent batteries. A white colonial town hall and a four-roomed brick schoolhouse were its only architectural distinctions. The mill once stood on the creek with its large mill pond and dam. The owner's large lacy Victorian house with tower, carriage house and caretaker's cottage lay across the creek. It's now a town museum stocked expensively with a fortune in plush Victorian furniture and tours guided by well-to-do volunteers. Minnetonka City now sprawls over forty square miles with fire stations, garbage pickup, sports club, golf courses, shopping malls and chain saws.

Into this once rural Eden, the peregrinations of restless urbanites anxious for the good country life on quarter acre lots with mature trees took land where only graying farmhouses and barns once stood. Driveways are crowded with RV's, van conversions and Volvos parked next to block-long Winnebagos, powerboats and snowmobiles under tarps.

From the top of our tallest elm, one could, in my youth, see the twenty-five story Foshay tower in the distance, the tallest building between Chicago and the West Coast. Cars once sparse on dusty township or blacktopped country roads were mostly Fords and Chevys that now have been replaced by Hondas, BMW's, and Mercedes. When I was a kid, the only large cars were the Buicks and Cadillacs and one regal olive green Rolls Royce with its chauffeur. They had fenders like battleship plate and belonged to the folks who lived in the great lakeside houses at Deephaven, Orono, and Wayzata. These were the "old rich" who owned the Minnetonka Yacht Club on its private island and lived behind wrought iron gates that fronted huge rambling houses with rose gardens, swimming pools, live-in maids and gardeners. They swooshed by daily--the Heffelfingers, Crosbys, Pillsburys, and Daytons--to plush offices or to concerts by Eugene Ormandy and the Minneapolis Symphony, the Arts Institute, galas at the Minneapolis Club or dinner at Charlie's Café Exceptionale.

Ours were homemade pleasures of oil barrel rafts on the spring-swollen creek, skiing by moonlight with homemade harnesses of screen door springs or cut inner tube bands. Our thrills were tandem skiing behind a Model-A Ford in the ditches of country roads, the only hazard being mailboxes or buried culverts. We swam in nearby gravel pits wading through peanut-buttery mud settled from gravel washing to deep clear water. Now our haunts are criss-crossed by a confusion of roads called Shadyridge Lane, Birchmont Drive, or Oakvale Circle and houses marked by fey signs announcing Blue Jay Perch, Cardinal Haven or Hawks' Rest.

Our mail was RFD, the flag up on the box for letters to mail or notes for three-cent stamps. We looked forward to the spring and fall Sear's catalogs thick as Chicago phone books with their racy pictures of models in "foundation garments," neat toys and alluring tools. One could furnish or even build a house from the Sear's "Dream Book." We ordered baby chicks in ventilated cartons delivered by mail to grow to fryers which supplemented our home grown and purely organic vegetable and fruit preserves. We picked bushels of windfall apples from abandoned orchards and sold them along the highway for two bits a bag to country-hungry city folks out for Sunday drives. We picked raspberries for two cents a quart for Bohemian berry farmers who truck-farmed around Hopkins, the "Raspberry Capital of the World." Pails of tart, black choke cherries and wild grapes became jams, jellies and syrup. The Hennepin County Fair provided risqué thrills and cheap carnival "girlie" shows where for additional dimes, additional articles of cover, already scant, would be removed in the sweaty tent redolent with the hog and sheep barns next door.

I look back to riding with my grandfather on Saturdays with horse and buckboard wagon two and a half miles to Hopkins for boxes of groceries and dusty bags of chick mash. The patient horse would be anchored with a twenty-five pound horse weight while I explored the wonders of town and my grandfather caught up with news at the feed elevator. Two cows kept us in milk and thick cream, which we blended with egg yolk-heavy custard. That went into the hand cranked freezer packed with salt and ice crushed in a burlap bag. Hagen-Daz could not touch its vanilla richness.

Once a week, the iceman cometh leaving thirty-pound chunks of lake ice tonged into our back porch icebox, the melt water dripped in a slimy stream to the ground below. Chicken dredged in flour, fried in lard on the three-burner oil stove together with home grown leaf lettuce, sweet corn, green beans and peas with mashed potatoes were featured at each Sunday dinner followed by wild strawberries from the marsh and thick cream and sugar. We didn't know there was a Depression.

Our house was homesteaded and built by my grandfather in 1872. It had electricity-bare bulbs on a ceiling cord, but no indoor plumbing or running water. It was years before we rewired it for floor plugs and our first "bridge lamp." The outhouse was well supplied with orange wrappers, a can of lime, and a sticky fly strip studded with dead flies like old raisins. Orange crates made good wren houses and kindling for the old four lidded cast iron cook stove which was relegated to the back stoop where wash water was heated in the large copper tub. Now the only horses are sleek thoroughbreds with English saddles, tied tails and wrapped legs ridden only on Sundays at shows at the Minnetonka Country Club or in exotic polo games at Wayzata. The old copper wash tubs now stand full of geraniums on suburban front steps.

School was in the four-room, eight-grade building run by a spinster principal, who also taught seventh and eighth grades, preparing us for the dreaded State Board examinations in arithmetic, social sciences, history, English and geography. The school contained a small but continually renewed branch of the Hennepin County Library System providing us with the National Geographic, Colliers, Popular Mechanics and the Saturday Evening Post from which we read stories by Faulkner, Hemingway, Cobb, and Lardner before we even knew they were famous. Assiduous perusal of geographic maps enabled me to ace the State Boards in geography. Now the greatly expanded school is a community center with exercise rooms jammed with glitzy equipment, a computer room, a host of social services, and a parking lot where our skating rink had been--not a Hudson, Essex, Nash or Studebaker in sight.

Nostalgia is of course nothing but the smoldering of ebbing memory, but memories bespeak, if not an easier way of life, nevertheless, a less hectic, complex and confusing one unaccelerated by TV, computers, credit cards and cash machines. We survived the Great Depression, WPA, and NRA crammed with cheap macaroni and cheese, stuffed beef heart, which when sliced revealed the ishy O's of ventricles and auricles, liver nearly free at the butchers, and a medley of homegrown and preserved foods with no vitamin content listed on the label.

We swam in the creek, skated in the winter dodging air holes under the ice, fired off tons of cherry bombs and pipe lengths, jammed with gravel, and giant firecrackers. We shot at each other with Roman candles and rockets of "farmer matches" in our BB guns which flamed with a load bang when they hit the target, once almost burning down the hay shed. Our worst job was on occasion to clean out the septic tank with an old WWI German helmet on a long pole, which was never long enough to stave off the disgusting stench below.

Our neighbors were farther apart with only distant barkings of farmyard dogs or the squeaking of windmills to give them away. Mornings we were awakened by crowing roosters or the rusty-pulled-nail screech of pheasants crossing the yard. We knew every car that went by except on Sundays when city folk "took a drive in the country" in newly washed cars. My grandfather on those days would sit on the front porch with his cigar and coffee can spittoon with his old cronies counting cars. One evening, he exclaimed with satisfaction, "Seventy-four today, a new record!" Now, cars by the hundreds pass in daily commuter scrambles to Dain Bosworth, ADM, Pillsbury, General Mills, American Express, numerous law firms and Norwest Bank.

We thought malls were what Joe Louis did to opponents as we listened avidly to radio broadcasts of the matches. We lived without K-Mart, transistors, CD's, dish antennae, power steering or Maalox. We lay before the walnut veneered tall Philco with its green Magic Eye tuner listening to Lux Radio Theater, the Ford Sunday Evening Hour, Ma Perkins, One Man's Family and Jack

Armstrong, All American Boy. On Saturdays, we reconstructed Bernie Bierman's Golden Gophers and the burly exploits of Bronco Nagurski, Pug Lund, and Ed Widseth skillfully given play by play by Halsey Hall and his joyous expletive "Holy Cow!" Our only radio news was Lowell Thomas, Cedric Adams and Roosevelt's Fireside chats.

Fall saw the itinerant threshing machine with its flapping belt joining tractor and separator belching out dusty mountains of glistening oat straw. Corn was still shocked by hand, and we looked for field mice nests squirming with blind, naked babies. The old milk cans we trundled to the roadside each day have been Martha Stewartized with painted daisies now holding canes and umbrellas.

Were times simpler in Minnetonka Mills? Perhaps they only seemed so in the unstructured days of our youth with no need for community recreational programs with full-time instructors. No one needed to instruct us how to use the woods, the gravel pit, build tree shacks high in the great elms or read reviews of the movies at the Hopkins Theater.

There for a quarter, one had Thursday Bank Nights with $100 drawings and Saturday matinees of "Tarzan the Ape-Man" or "The Last of the Mohicans." Then the feature began with preferably Laurel and Hardy, Irene Dunne, Tom Mix or John Barrymore larger than life. Halcyon days? Without a doubt. But as we grew beyond pastoral pleasures, headed for college or Dunwoody Technical School to learn sheet metal work or to pump gas at Ernie's, through the War and marriage we lost something--a life without open spaces out our back door, equanimity and closely bonded friendships. We did not need drug counseling, want crisis intervention, witness driveby shootings or experience road rage. We lived without Carnival Cruises, frontal nudity on TV, snowmobiles and roads glutted with conversion vans, box-car-sized semis, UPS trucks, empty beer cans and plastic bags cluttering the roadsides.

We were amazed when Highway 7 from Minneapolis to Excelsior was widened into a four lane "freeway" with cloverleaf intersections and overpasses. In the Land of 10,000 Lakes, "up North" meant two weeks in a frame cabin with bare studs, iron cots, a Coleman lantern, mosquitoes, and the ubiquitous three burner oil stove smelling of fish fried in bacon grease, and an outdoor privy swarming with chipmunks. Now the North Country is loaded with posh condos fronting 18 hole golf courses, supper clubs, sports bars with fifty-inch TV's, and humongous resorts at $200 per night. One has to go nearly to Canada to hear a loon cry, the splash of a lunker pike in night waters or the screech of oar locks on a cedar bottomed rowboat.

What have we lost? Perhaps a warmth and depth of relationships to nature and each other and attachment to place, the local grocery with its brass cash register next to a glass-doomed wheel of sharp cheddar cheese bought by the wedge, free Popsicle sticks treasured until we could treat our friends, Ernie's garage, our YMCA with its tales of fast girls, "dirty" jokes, and smoking ten cent a pack Avalons around the iron wood stove. The fastest thrill around was the roller coaster at Excelsior Amusement Park which is now condominiums with Jacuzzis and a huge marina where city folks gather on weekends to drink martinis and play bridge on their anchored cabin cruisers as large as the QE II. Missing are the night barking dogs, pigeons cooing on the barn roof, barn swallows nest building with mud under the eaves, a real telephone operator to take your number from the crank phone, and long sleeps on rainy Saturday mornings. Gone is the clashing hand-pushed lawn mower, fragrant alfalfa glistening with morning dew, pasture burning and leaves falling. Then was a pace that defied heart palpitations, acid reflux, and fume-filled lungs.

What have we gained? Perhaps only things of great value but little worth. Our cars have more horsepower than a hundred farm horses. We consume tons of salsa and Taco chips, double whoppers, Dairy Queens, fresh salmon fillets at $10 a pound and Red Barron Pizza. Our weekly grocery bills would have kept us for a month. Are we better for dot com and a world of billionaire entrepreneurs and overpaid and over muscled football players who could have paid off the national debt in our youth? No. We are just older, somewhat jaded by the advent of a new millennium and prone to reflection on our Minnesota that's fast disappearing.

The great elm with its five-foot girth outside my childhood bedroom window still stands, a sold anchor and testament to the past. On my porch hangs my grandfather's last horse bridle with its cracked leather blinders and rusty bit, a heavy iron horse shoe with ice lugs and a wood pulley from the hayloft fork. Thomas Wolfe once wrote, "You can't go home again." Reluctantly, Thomas, I must agree. It's not there any longer.

Graham Frear taught English at Northfield High School before becoming an Irish scholar and English Professor Emeritus at St. Olaf College in Northfield, Minnesota.

Kathy Megyeri graduated from Owatonna High School and taught secondary English for 34 years in Maryland. She is currently an education consultant in Washington, D. C. In 1995, she won the Distinguished Alumna Award from her alma mater, St. Olaf College in Northfield, MN. Her formative years living in the Land of 10,000 Lakes have provided her with a multitude of stories in her other career as a writer.

Joan Claire Graham graduated from Albert Lea High School, where she was profoundly influenced by journalism teacher Edna Gercken and theatre director Wally Kennedy. Since graduating from Winona State in 1967, Joan has taught high school English, speech, drama, and journalism, has written and directed plays, has directed a cooperative nursery school, and has written family histories and freelance articles. The mother of two incredibly talented, beautiful and intelligent adult daughters, Joan lives in Maryland.

The authors invite you to submit your Minnesota Memory for Volume 2. You may email submissions to Megyeri@Juno.com or to MinnMemory@aol.com.

To order additional copies, contact Graham Megyeri Books, 3227-22 University Blvd. W., Kensington, Maryland 20895, Phone 301-942-3183 or contact the writers at MinnMemory@aol.com

.